CAROL VORDERMAN

HELP YOUR KIDS WITH

SATs

KEY STAGE 2

FOREWORD

Every year, for a week in May, Year 6 children are expected to take a series of tests, known as SATs papers. SATs is an abbreviation for Standard Attainment Tests. Children will be tested in Maths, Reading, and SPaG (Spelling, Punctuation, and Grammar) in timed tests, which are sent away to be marked externally. The results are declared to parents usually by the end of the summer term, and often included in the end of year report. The results are given as a set of scaled scores, with 80 being the lowest and 120 being the highest. Any score of 100 or over is considered a pass.

In addition to this, your child will receive a set of teacher assessments for Maths, Reading, Writing, and Science. These are the grades awarded by the teacher, having assessed your child over a period of time. The subjects will be graded according to the school's grading system, which should be explained in the report. The grades will indicate whether your child has reached the expected standard, above the expected standard, or below the expected standard for each of those subjects. Teachers have been given a framework for teacher assessments and will almost certainly have attended training on this topic. The Local Authority will also moderate some schools on their assessments, though the schools selected varies year on year.

The advice in this book is specifically aimed at supporting children through the tests, but all of it is relevant for the final year at primary school. The first chapter provides reassurance about the tests and practical advice for keeping your child calm through this time. In the other chapters, there are pages explaining what will be in each of the tests, as well as reference and practice pages to reinforce and support preparation for the tests in schools.

HELP YOUR KIDS WITH

SATs

KEY STAGE 2

Consultant
Jacqueline Harris

Written by Peter Clarke, Caroline Clissold, John Hesk, John Kennedy,
Cherri Moseley, Jacqueline Harris, Sheila Dignen, Claire White
Consultants Peter Clarke, Matt Grant, Claire Langford,
Sean McArdle, Amy O'Connor, Claire White
Editorial team Anwesha Dutta, Vineetha Mokkil
Design team Jaileen Kaur, Nehal Verma
Managing Editors Deborah Lock, Alka Thakur
Managing Art Editors Diane Peyton Jones, Romi Chakraborty
Senior DTP Designer Shanker Prasad
CTS Manager Balwant Singh

Material in this publication was previously published in
Help Your Kids with Study Skills (2011); *English Made Easy* (Key Stage 2: Ages 9–10, 2014);
English Made Easy (Key Stage 2: Ages 10–11, 2015);
Visual Guide to Grammar and Puntuation (2017); *Spell Check* (2017);
Spelling, Punctuation & Grammar Made Easy (KS2 Higher: Ages 10–11, 2015);
How to be Good at Maths (2016);
Maths Made Easy (Key Stage 2 Advanced: Ages 10–11, 2014);
Maths Made Easy (Key Stage 2 Beginner: Ages 10–11, 2016)

First published in Great Britain in 2017 by Dorling Kindersley Limited
80 Strand, London WC2R 0RL

Copyright © 2011, 2014, 2015, 2016, 2017 Dorling Kindersley Limited
A Penguin Random House Company
002—309469—Dec/2017

A CIP catalogue record for this book is available from the British Library.
ISBN: 978-0-2413-3594-9

Printed and bound in China

A WORLD OF IDEAS
SEE ALL THERE IS TO KNOW

www.dk.com

CONTENTS

 HANDLING ANXIETY

Reassurance about SATs   10
Coping with thepressure of SATs 12
Calming exercises   14
Time out   16
Learning styles   18
Helping your child learn   20

2 READING

Reading test   24
Preparing for the Reading test 26
Reading a text   28
A traditional story   30
Understanding poetry   32
Letter of complaint   34
Reading a classic novel   36
Reading another classic novel   38
Fast fact-finding   40
Following instructions   41
Non-fiction writing   42
Onomatopoeia   43

Present and past tenses   54
Future tense   55
Progressive tenses   56
Perfect tenses   58
Infinitives   60
Adjectives   62
Adverbs   64
Comparatives and superlatives   66
Prepositions   68
Prepositions of place   69
Coordinating conjunctions   70
Subordinating conjunctions   71
Interjections   72
Determiners   74
Statements   76
Questions   77
Exclamations   78
Commands   79
Noun phrases   80
Prepositional phrases   81
Adverbials   82
Fronted adverbials   83

3 SPELLING, PUNCTUATION AND GRAMMAR

SPaG tests   46
Preparing for the SPaG tests   48
Proper nouns   50
Abstract nouns   51
Pronouns   52

Antonyms	124
Antonyms: using a prefix	125
Punctuation: getting it right!	126
Advanced punctuation	127
Colons and semi-colons in lists	128
Ellipses	130
Parenthesis: using brackets	131
Bullet points	132
Apostrophe to show possession	133
Homophones	134
Words with "ie" and "ei"	135
Direct speech	136
Reported speech	137
Formal and informal speech	138
Points of view	140
Personification	141
Exploring synonyms	142
Synonyms for "said"	143
Types of sentence	144
Clauses and connectives	145
Active and passive	146
Paragraphs and punctuation	147

Clauses	84
Main clauses	86
Subordinate clauses	88
Relative clauses	89
Relative pronouns	90
Active and passive sentences	92
Direct speech	94
Reported speech	95
Capital letters	96
Full stops	97
Question marks	98
Exclamation marks	99
Commas	100
Apostrophes	102
Possessive apostrophes	103
Colons	104
Semi-colons	105
Sing a spelling	106
Does it look right?	108
Hopping around letters	110
An elephant never forgets	112
How to remember the echidna	114
Watch out for the rat!	116
Word art	118
Silent consonants	120
Root words	121
Prefixes	122
Suffixes	123

4 MATHS

Maths test	150
Preparing for the Maths test	152
Positive and negative numbers	154
Rounding	156
Factors	158
Multiples	160
Prime numbers	162
Adding fractions	164
Subtracting fractions	165
Multiplying fractions	166
Dividing fractions	168
Comparing and ordering decimals	170

Rounding decimals	171		Add and subtract fractions	201
Calculating percentages	172		Multiply fractions	202
Ratio	174		Divide fractions	203
Proportion	175		Ratio and proportion	204
The order of operations	176		Algebra	205
Nets	178		Decimal addition	206
Using a protractor	180		Problems with negative numbers	207
Angles inside polygons	182		Real life problems	208
Calculating the angles in a polygon	183		Simple use of brackets	209
			Multiplying decimals	210
Positive and negative coordinates	184		Division by units	211
Using coordinates to draw a polygon	185		Division of 3-digit decimal numbers	212
Averages	186		Real-life problems	213
The mean	187		Reading from scales	214
Line graphs	188		Mean, median, and mode	215
Pie charts	190		Multiplying decimals	216
Solving equations	192		Real-life problems	218
Formulas and sequences	194		Fraction problems	220
Two-dimensional shapes	196		Finding percentages	221
Three-dimensional shapes	197		More algebra	222
Multiplication tables	198		Multiplication by tens and units	223
Factors, multiples, and prime numbers	200		Naming parts of a circle	224
			Area of right-angled triangles	225
			Cubes of small numbers	226
			Cubes of larger numbers	227
			Nets of 3D shapes	228
			Nets of simple shapes	229
			Drawing angles including reflex	230
			Drawing more angles including reflex	231
			Drawing 2D shapes	232
			Coordinates	233
			Answers	234
			Index	254
			Acknowledgements	256

Handling anxiety

Reassurance about SATs

WANTING YOUR CHILD TO DO WELL IN TESTS IS NATURAL, BUT TRUST THAT THE SCHOOL IS PREPARING YOUR CHILD WELL.

The pressure of SATs can be a stressful time for parents. It is important not to show your anxiety as this will lead to your child becoming anxious, too. Here is some reassurance about SATs and the results.

Perspective

SATs are used more to measure the school rather than an individual child. The school inspectors, OFSTED, and the Local Education Authority look at SATs and compare schools based on the results.

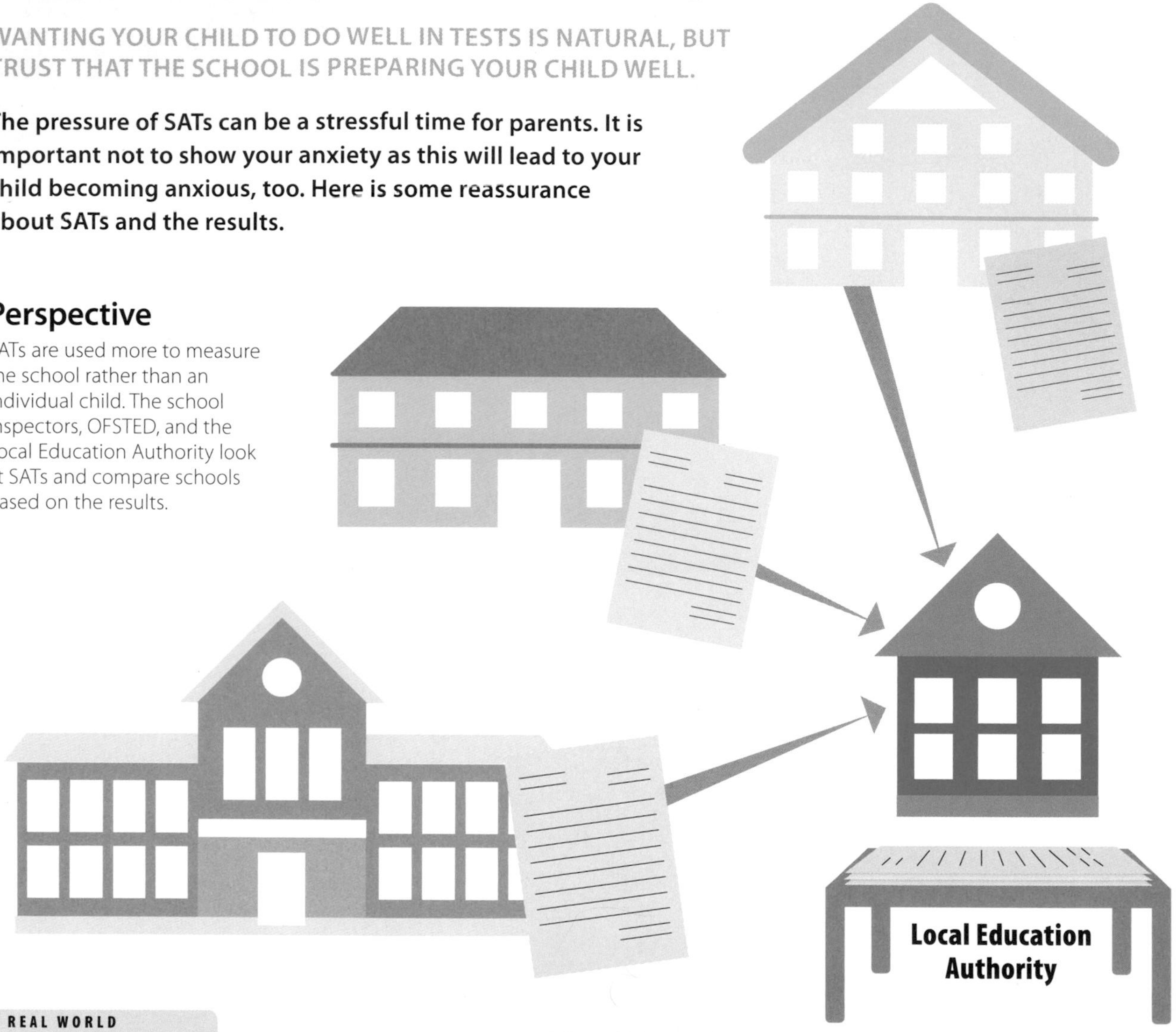

REAL WORLD

Special needs

Schools plan in advance for access arrangements for children with disabilities or special educational needs. Access arrangements for SATs are based on normal classroom practice, for example, using a sloping desk to write or a coloured overlay or large print copies. In a few cases, extra time or a reader for maths are arranged.

"The tests are **not qualifications** and don't affect your child's future options in school."
Standards & Testing Agency

Snapshot

SATs only measure a child's performance on that day. For some children this is fine, but for other children things happen that day that can affect their results. If this is the case, the teacher assessment is a much better guide to achievement. Each SATs paper is like a quick photo of a moment. Sometimes a fantastic photo is taken and sometimes it is terrible. The subject of the photo is still the same.

▷ Teacher assessment
Your child's teacher will have worked all year to monitor your child's progress and achievement over a longer period of time. This is a far more reliable assessment of your child's abilities at this age.

Expectations

Every child is different and everyone is good at different things. Your child will perform differently to others in the class or a sibling in the SATS, so it's very important not to compare or impose expectations.

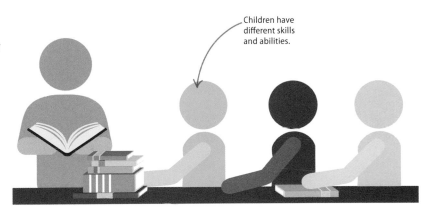

Children have different skills and abilities.

▷ Challenging expectations
We don't expect children to be the same height, so we can't expect them to all get exactly the same results. Some children are skilled at football, while others prefer reading books, or excel at playing an instrument or painting a picture.

Future

Your child's SATs results will not impact on secondary school. Children will already have their school places and the results do not change that. Also many secondary schools retest children when they start, as they recognise that SATs results can be unreliable.

"It is very unlikely that **Year 6 SATs** results are ever asked about in later **schooling**"

Coping with the pressure of SATs

MAINTAINING YOUR CHILD'S WELLBEING IS A KEY PART TO PREPARING HIM OR HER FOR THE SATS.

Children may find themselves under great pressure in the lead up to their SATs. Here are some ways to help your child cope and stay calm through this time.

Sleep matters

Make sure your child gets lots of early nights. Ensure screens and TVs are turned off before bedtime as these can disrupt sleep patterns. If your child is having trouble sleeping, a warm bath with lavender or a warm milky drink are both calming and relaxing.

Try to sleep for at least nine hours.

Exercise

Fresh air and activity are a great help for getting a good night's sleep and feeling good about yourself.

REAL WORLD

Physical activity

The brain produces feel-good chemicals during activities such as swimming or running. Physical activity also pushes more oxygen around the body, including to the brain, which helps it to work better.

Eating healthily

Diet has an impact on concentration. Eating breakfast is particularly important, but it needs to have a long-lasting effect. Sugar makes us feel full of life to begin with but then causes a slump in energy before the next meal. Porridge, fruit, and brown bread provide a steady supply of energy. SATs papers are often in the morning, so a good breakfast is key.

▷ **Energy for the brain**
The brain uses 20 per cent of all our energy, and needs regular feeding.

Fruit is an ideal snack.

Experts recommend five portions of fruit and vegetables a day.

Reassuring words

Tell your child that you understand what they are going through, and love them, regardless of the results. Just ask them to do their best and make it clear you are relaxed about the outcome and trust them. Parts of the SATs papers can sometimes not be as expected, but children who are confident that their parents understand, will do their best and not get upset by these questions.

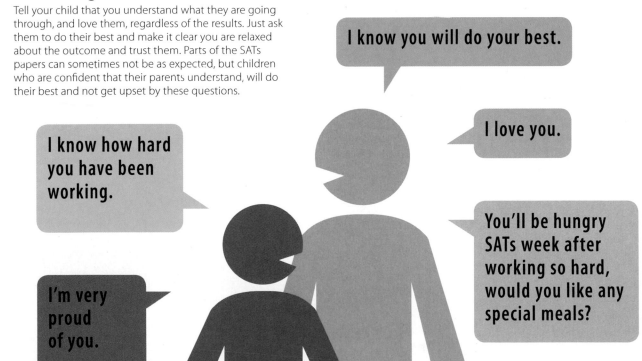

I know you will do your best.

I love you.

I know how hard you have been working.

I'm very proud of you.

You'll be hungry SATs week after working so hard, would you like any special meals?

13

Calming exercises

IF YOUR CHILD FEELS PANICKY DURING THE SATS, HE OR SHE CAN USE SOME RELAXATION TECHNIQUES.

Show and try out with your child a few simple relaxation techniques. These will slow down the breathing, which calms any panic.

> "**Pause** for a moment, **breathe**, **focus** on the breath. **Know** that you are **OK**, in this moment."
> Leo Babauta (b. 1973), Zenhabits.net founder and author

Relaxing through breathing

Panic can often lead to shallow or "low-volume" breathing, which means that the body is getting rid of more carbon dioxide than usual. This affects the blood and body functions, and can increase anxiety. Learning how to control breathing is an effective way to maintain both carbon dioxide and oxygen levels. It is the easiest way to reduce anxiety and calm down, and will help with concentration and increase energy. We need to take in deeper and slower breaths by breathing "into our stomach".

1. Put your hands on the chest and belly.

2. Inhale into the belly, so that the hand on the belly moves, but not the hand on the chest.

3. Count to six while breathing in. Hold the breath for a few moments, then breathe out for a count of six.

After continuing this exercise for several minutes, you should notice that you are becoming more relaxed.

▷ **Deep breathing**
Taking tests requires concentration, effort, and makes a lot of demands on the brain. Show your child how to breathe deeply. If he or she practises this technique daily, it will soon become a natural process. It will be useful before any performance, too.

7/11 breathing technique

This breathing technique instantly reduces high anxiety levels and can prevent children from having a panic attack during stressful moments, such as during the test. It involves breathing in while counting to seven, and breathing out for a count of 11. If this is too much, children can try breathing in to the count of five and out to seven or eight. Breathing out for longer than breathing in helps to switch the body from the sympathetic nervous system, which responds to stress, to the parasympathetic nervous system, which is responsible for relaxation and calmness.

▷ **Focus on the body**
When we concentrate on our breathing, it means we are not thinking of anything else during that period. Therefore, we are able to calm down.

1. Breathe in while counting 1–7. Notice the belly expand.

2. Breathe out while counting 1–11. Notice the belly pulling in again.

3. Repeat the process for several minutes.

Alternative techniques

Some alternative techniques, such as the Emotional Freedom Technique (EFT), are effective for releasing stress. EFT involves tapping on certain body points, using one or two fingers, while expressing anxious feelings out loud. Often, the feelings shift very quickly, especially when they are expressed verbally. Tapping releases the energy behind the stress and helps us to calm down. Using this technique, we can tap away negative emotions, such as stress and anxiety. It is safe and really easy to learn, and can be done with friends and family.

2. Top of the head

3. Beginning of the eyebrow (either on the left or right or both sides)

4. Side of the eye (either on the left or right or both sides)

5. Under the eye

6. Under the nose

7. Under the lips

9. Top of each finger, by the nailbed

8. Collarbone point

▷ **EFT tapping**
Each body point is tapped for a few seconds – in the correct order, from 1 to 9 – while a negative feeling is described. Focus on the feelings throughout the exercise.

1. Tap lightly with one or two fingers on the side of the hand.

Go on an inner journey

Another way to relax is to engage one's imagination and go on an "inner journey". Children can imagine a safe space in their mind, where they can feel calm and happy. They could imagine a holiday spot that they have been to, create a scene of their own, or use an inspiring picture from a magazine. In that safe place, children can forget about the tests and have fun in their imaginary world.

Sit comfortably or lie down.

Children can "stay" in the imaginary place for as long as they like.

Create an imaginary place in the mind, such as a forest glade.

Use the senses: notice the colours, smells, sounds, and other sensations in that place.

◁ **Inner journey**
Children should go on an inner journey each week, letting their imagination take them to their favourite places of relaxation.

15

Time out

DOING SOMETHING YOUR CHILD ENJOYS WILL TAKE
HIS OR HER MIND OFF THE SATS.

Your child will be working very hard at school and will need
a break. This is particularly important on the weekend
before the SATs. Laughing and having fun is key.

Get inspired and energized

A car cannot run at full speed forever – it needs to stop
and refuel. The same is true for learners. Children need
to take breaks to recharge their batteries. Going out
and meeting friends are pleasant shared activities that
will provide the reboost before the SATs begin.

Playing sport with friends

▽ **Take a break**
Time out activities can range from day
excursions to sports events, playing music,
or baking. After an afternoon of pursuing
hobbies or meeting friends, it is likely that
children will feel inspired and energized.

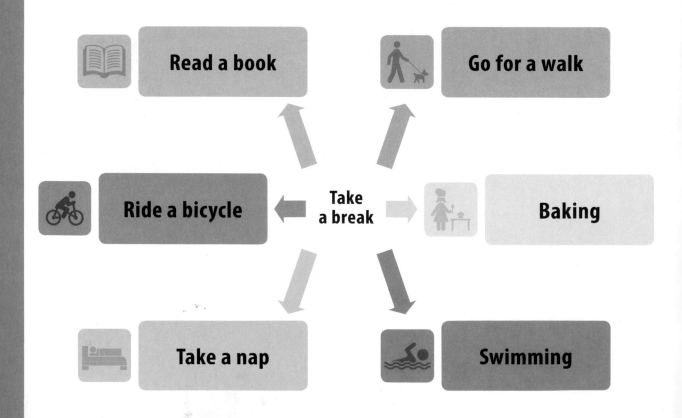

Find real-life applications

Sometimes, being out and about helps with making connections to what has been learnt. Visiting famous places, monuments, or museums can provide plenty to talk and read about, while going to a park, a forest, or a zoo can be opportunities to apply some practical maths. You and your child can also find your own examples and real-life applications elsewhere, such as in the home or outside in the country.

▷ **Search for examples**
Be creative when looking for real-life applications. This makes learning more interesting and helps in understanding and remembering things better.

Find examples of items in lesson topics (e.g. fungi for biology) and take pictures to support notes.

Keep a notebook and pen handy for recording observations.

Reading together

Reading to your child or listening together to stories or plays on the radio and audio books are pleasant activities. They also provide the chance to talk about a story and think about what has been written, which is a useful skill for the SATs reading paper.

"**Learning** is an **experience. Everything** else is **just information.**"
Albert Einstein (1879–1955), Physicist

Use hobbies as memory triggers

A hobby can also be used to practise what your child is learning. A different environment can be a powerful memory trigger when trying to remember certain aspects of a topic. Parts of the hobby routine, or the people involved, could be mentally connected with the items to be learnt.

▷ **Memory trigger**
Children should imagine a scenario in which they can connect the information to the hobby, and they can try to remember the details while engaged in the activity. Here, the names of different football players are linked to maths 2D shapes.

Peter (**P**entagon) **S**teve (**S**quare) **O**scar (**O**ctagon) **H**enry (**H**exagon) **T**im (**T**riangle) **R**obin (**R**ectangle)

Pentagon Square Octagon Hexagon Triangle Rectangle

Learning styles

CHILDREN LEARN IN DIFFERENT WAYS. KNOWING THIS
CAN HELP YOU WORK OUT HOW TO HELP THEM BEST.

Traditional teaching methods tend to use mostly verbal and
logical approaches. In recent years, educators have started to
recognize that children learn in a wider variety of ways.

Since most children **learn**
in **multiple ways**, it is **best**
to present **information** in
multiple ways.

Social

Social learners are skilled
communicators and are good
at listening to other people's
views. They enjoy bouncing
their ideas off other people
and working through issues
within a group. Outside the
classroom, social learners may
like to role-play different
points of view.

"I don't know
where to start!"

"Let's brainstorm
together."

"I'll mind map
our ideas."

▷ **Group dynamics**
Let your child share his
or her ideas and explain
the homework with family
members and friends. Make
sure everyone takes their turn.

Solitary

Solitary learners are independent and focus well
when they study alone. They may find group
work frustrating and unhelpful. These learners
are good at setting goals for themselves and
may find it useful to keep a learning journal to
assess the effectiveness of their study methods.
However, they should recognize that if they
get stuck on an issue, it may be a good idea
to talk it through with others.

◁ **A questioning attitude**
It can be useful for independent
learners to ask themselves
questions, which may stimulate
the thinking process.

It is fine for children to do their
homework in a quiet spot on
their own, but they should
remember not to be isolated
the whole time.

A range of techniques

Some people prefer a particular learning style, while others find that a mixture of styles works best for them. It may also depend on the subject. The ways in which children learn best can also change over time.

▽ **Mix your styles**
Each learning style uses different sections of the brain. The most effective learning styles engage many parts of the brain at the same time.

Logical

These learners are good at maths and work through problems in a logical way. They recognize patterns and links, and can group together related pieces of information. They make lists of things to do, ranking them in order.

Verbal

These learners are comfortable expressing themselves through speech and writing. They are avid readers, with a good vocabulary. Verbal learners can benefit by using speaking, writing, rhythm, and rhyme when learning information.

Visual

Visual learners have good spatial awareness and enjoy drawing – they often doodle while learning. These learners like using pictures, mind maps, and diagrams to organize information. Colour-coding can be used to highlight different themes.

Logical

Visual   Verbal

LEARNING STYLES

Aural   Physical

Aural

Aural learners probably play a musical instrument and enjoy singing. They learn best through active listening, by taking part in discussions, or by using audio clips. They like to use sound, music, rhythm, and rhyme in their learning.

Physical

These learners tend to like being active and find it helpful to think through problems while exercising. To learn how something works, they would prefer to take it apart than read the instructions.

Helping your child learn

HAVING A FAMILY MEMBER HELPING CAN MAKE
ALL THE DIFFERENCE TO A CHILD'S ACHIEVEMENT.

To successfully help your child, you should adopt a positive attitude, an open mind to new methods, and be prepared to join in with the activities.

Attitude

It can be particularly challenging to work with your child, so it is important for you to have the right attitude. Stay calm and positive, and try to keep a neutral tone – it is advisable not to share negative learning experiences. Build a positive attitude by keeping the times short.

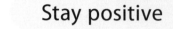

Keep calm

Stay positive

▷ **The right mindset**
A helper needs to remain calm and supportive, and encourage a positive attitude towards learning.

"Follow the general advice **teachers** give about supporting your child's learning **throughout the year.**"
Standards & Testing Agency

△ **Learning apps**
These apps allow children to study on the go. For example, apps are available on smartphones for practising vocabulary and grammar.

◁ **E-learning**
E-learning enables children to access the curriculum remotely. Often, they can communicate with teachers and other children online.

Teaching methods

You will probably find that teaching methods have changed significantly since you were at school. Subjects may be taught differently and methods of assessment have changed. A variety of new technologies are used – for example, learning apps can be downloaded onto smartphones, children use tablets in class, and many learning materials are available from websites.

◁ **Websites**
A wide range of learning materials can be found online. Children will be recommended websites by their school teachers.

Learning together

Learning with another person can be productive and enjoyable, and it stimulates thinking. When a person shares their knowledge with someone else, it helps to clarify his or her own thoughts and to embed the concepts and methods involved. Explaining an idea can spark off further ideas, too. Children gain from their helper's experience, knowledge, and different points of view.

▽ **Child as teacher**
This child is learning about grammar. He or she needs to explain to the helper that the "fronted adverbial" describes how, why, when, or where something happens at the start of a sentence.

The teacher says I need to write fronted adverbials.

The child understands the term and will need to explain it to the helper.

What on earth is a fronted adverbial?

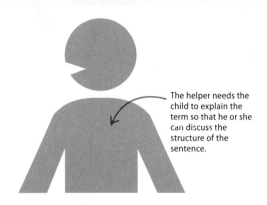

The helper needs the child to explain the term so that he or she can discuss the structure of the sentence.

Feedback

It is very important to help keep children motivated by giving them feedback. It is best to balance praise with constructive criticism. The "sandwich" approach works well. Start with positive comments, then indicate what could be improved, focusing on the main issues and being as specific as possible – no learner wants to be bombarded with a long list of things to correct. Finally, it is good to offer further positive comments to end the discussion on a good note.

More positive feedback: round off with further praise

▷ **Feedback sandwich**
Even if the work needs a lot of improvement, a helper should praise the effort that a child has made or the fact that he or she completed the homework or activity on time.

Tips for improvement: focus on the main issues

Positive feedback: list a few good points

"Whatever the **difference** between **brilliant** and **average brains**, we are all **creative**. And through **practice** and **study** we can **enhance** our **skills**."
Jeff Hawkins (b. 1957), Inventor

Reading

Reading test

CHILDREN'S READING ABILITY IS TESTED BY
A ONE-HOUR PAPER.

The reading test assesses children's ability to read, understand, and make conclusions from fiction, non-fiction, and poetry. They are given three texts to read.

"Pupils should be taught to **read fluently**, understand extended prose (both fiction and non-fiction) and be encouraged to **read for pleasure**."

The National Curriculum, 2013

Extracts

Children are given an illustrated booklet. This contains three different texts, which are extracts from fiction, poetry, and non-fiction writing. The pieces get progressively harder.

Questions

Children are given a separate answer booklet that contains the questions about each text. Most questions are worth one mark with some worth two marks and a very few worth three marks, requiring a longer answer. The length of the answer expected is shown by the amount of space given.

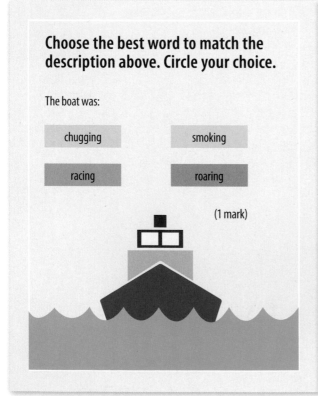

Choose the best word to match the description above. Circle your choice.

The boat was:

chugging   smoking

racing   roaring

(1 mark)

Number the following events 1-5 to show the order in which they happened. The first one has been done for you.

Gaby breaks the universal rule of tree climbing. [ ]

Gaby notices the cat. [1]

Gaby tries to pick up the cat. [ ]

Gaby remembers the water-balloon fight. [ ]

Gaby takes her cardigan off. [ ]

(1 mark)

△ **Multiple choice**
These require children to pick the word they think best describes an aspect of the text.

△ **Sequencing**
The text is summarised in a few sentences and children have to number them in the correct order.

▽ Matching and labelling

For non-fiction texts, children may be asked to draw lines to link the information, or to add labels.

▽ Extended questions

These questions require more deduction and reasoning. Children are asked to explain an opinion or talk about how the writer is using words to engage the reader. These types of questions ask for evidence from the text to support their answers.

Match the events below to the year in which they happened.

Anousheh Ansari went to space.	1969
The first man stepped on the Moon.	1998
Dennis Tito went to space.	2001
The International Space Station was built.	2006

(1 mark)

Look at page 5.

What are three ways the cat shows it does not enjoy Gaby trying to rescue it?

_____

_____

_____

_____

(2 marks)

Look at the paragraph beginning: Carefully, Michael leaned...

What does this paragraph tell you about Michael's character? Explain two features of his character, using evidence from the text to support your answer.

_____

_____

_____

_____

_____

_____

_____

(3 marks)

△ Short questions

These questions ask children to find and copy a word or phrase directly from the text that answers the question.

REAL WORLD

Which order?

The questions in the test do not have to be answered in order. Children can decide to start with the hardest ones first, when they are fresh. This may be useful for children with poor concentration or children who get tired. If this might be an issue for your child, then discuss what order will work best for him or her with the class teacher.

Preparing for the Reading test

OPPORTUNITIES TO READ TOGETHER AND TALK ABOUT BOOKS ARE ESSENTIAL.

Showing an interest in what your child is reading, and asking questions to help him or her see how wonderful it is to read will provide essential support as your child prepares for the reading test.

Reading for pleasure

Research shows that children who read for pleasure are found to do better at school, and this carries on into secondary school. It doesn't matter what your child is reading, so long as he or she is enjoying it. Any book or magazine about something your child is interested in, such as football or fashion, will get him or her engaged.

Ways to find a good read
Friend recommendations
Visit a library and ask a librarian
Access book lists for different ages

"The more that you **read**, the more **things** you will know. The more that you **learn**, the more **places** you'll go."

Dr Seuss, *I can read with my eyes shut!*

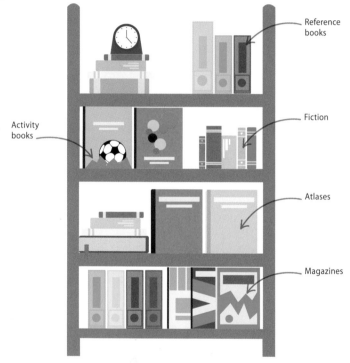

Reference books

Activity books

Fiction

Atlases

Magazines

Reading aloud

At any age, hear your child read aloud to you and check she or he understands what it's about. The speed at which children read influences their comprehension. Too slow and they may lose the thread of the text and forget what's happening; too fast and they are more likely to misread and misunderstand.

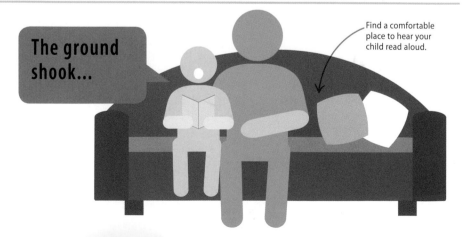

The ground shook...

Find a comfortable place to hear your child read aloud.

Asking in-depth questions

You can help support your child by asking questions about the books he or she is reading. This will help your child engage with reading and find evidence in the text.

What might happen next?

What are the key themes in this story and what makes you think that?

Why do you think the character acted as he did? What made you think that?

What would you think of this situation if you were in it?

What are the differences between the characters?

What other information would you need to know to understand this event better?

Which was the turning point in the story?

Would you be friends with this character and why?

What might be a more exciting title for this book?

Bedtime story

Spend some time reading with your child. This quality time will develop the pleasure of reading, and subsequently build the skills needed for SATs.

"Argh!" he cried...

Reading a text

Read this **text**, then answer the questions in full sentences.

The Voice of Nature

An Aboriginal myth from southern Australia relates how, in the beginning, the voice of the Ancestor spoke each day from a great gum tree, and the tribe gathered around to listen. But as time went by the people grew weary of hearing his words of wisdom. One by one they turned their backs on the voice to pursue their own pleasures, and a vast silence settled over the whole of the land and the sea. There was no wind and the tides were still, no birds sang, and the earth seemed to be dying.

The tribe soon wearied of the pleasures of their own making and began to be afraid and lonely. They returned to the great tree again and again, hoping to hear the words that would ease their misery. And one day the voice of their Ancestor spoke again.

He told them it was the last time his voice would be heard, but that he would give them a sign. The great tree split open, a huge tongue of light came down into its trunk, and then it closed up again.

Since that time the Aboriginals have known that the voice of their Ancestor exists in all things, and speaks to them through every part of nature.

From *Dreamtime Heritage* by A. & M. J. Roberts

Why did the tribe traditionally gather around the great gum tree?

To hear Wisdom

Why did the people abandon this custom (stop going to the tree)?

To Persue there own Pleasure

What happened to the natural world when the people broke this tradition?

It Sarted dieing to die

What feelings made the people return to the tree?

truth

Reading and understanding

Reread the **text** on page 28, then answer the following questions in full sentences. *die*

What is an **ancestor**? D

....

....

Describe the sign given to the people by the Ancestor. Explain the meaning of the sign.

....

....

....

The Australian gum tree has a **scientific** name. Use **reference books** or a **computer** to find out what it is, and write it here.

....

Explain the word **tribe**. What do we mean by **tribal society**? D

....

....

What evidence can you find in the text to suggest that **nature** was important to the people? Can you explain why this was?

....

....

Use a **dictionary** to find out what the saying "up a gum tree" means. D

....

....

....

What does this passage make you feel?
Which words make you feel like this?

....

....

....

Note: D means to use a dictionary for these practice pages.
In the actual test, children will not be able to use a dictionary.

A traditional story

Read this **story** from India about a tree, and answer the questions in full sentences. The writer explains that, as a child, she often heard this story told on a special day in August – the Day for Brothers – when "all sisters in India pray that no harm comes to their brothers".

The Mango Tree (Part One)

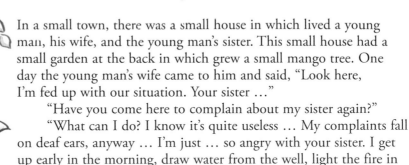

In a small town, there was a small house in which lived a young man, his wife, and the young man's sister. This small house had a small garden at the back in which grew a small mango tree. One day the young man's wife came to him and said, "Look here, I'm fed up with our situation. Your sister …"

"Have you come here to complain about my sister again?"

"What can I do? I know it's quite useless … My complaints fall on deaf ears, anyway … I'm just … so angry with your sister. I get up early in the morning, draw water from the well, light the fire in the kitchen, cook breakfast, wash and scrub pots …"

"Don't go on," said the brother. "I've heard it all before."

"And what does your lazy sister do all day? Nothing … nothing … she lolls about in the garden, watering her mango tree, talking to it, clearing away dead leaves, and feeding it manure and mulch …"

"That isn't all she does. She comes in and talks to me. Just an hour ago, she was playing chess with me."

"Just because she adores you, doesn't mean you should ignore her faults. You must tell her to leave that … silly mango tree alone, and come and help me with the housework. I think she needs to get married. That might teach her to be more responsible."

Since the sister was of marriageable age, the brother could not really object. He knew though, that he would miss her very, very much.

A marriage was planned.

Why did the young man's wife complain to him?

She spends to much time to the tree

Why did the wife think the sister should marry?

Now read part two of the **story** that began on page 30, then answer the questions.

The Mango Tree (Part Two)

When all the ceremonies were over, and the sister was about to leave with her groom to lead a new life in a new town, she turned to her sister-in-law and said, "Dearest sister-in-law, I'm going to miss my mango tree so much. Would you please do me a great favour and look after it for me? Please water it well and clear the weeds that grow in its shadow."

"Oh, well, yes, yes," answered the sister-in-law.

Once the sister had left, the sister-in-law turned to her husband and yelled, "Did you hear that? Did you *hear* that? Did you hear your selfish sister? She didn't say that she was going to miss you. She didn't say that she was going to miss me. She *did* say that she was going to miss her mango tree!" She decided then that she was going to ignore the mango tree. The mango tree irritated her just as much as her husband's sister had. Now she could be rid of both.

As the days passed, the unwatered, uncared for mango tree started drying up and its leaves began to fall.

At the same time, the brother, who had been a strong, robust and healthy young man, began to lose his appetite and get thinner and weaker.

One day, a letter arrived. It was from the sister and said, "Dearest brother and sister-in-law. I hope all is well and that my tree is green, and that my brother is in good health."

The remaining leaves of the mango tree were quite yellow by this time, but the sister-in-law wrote back, "Dearest sister. Your tree is fine, but your brother has not been feeling so good."

Soon another letter arrived from the sister. "Are you sure my tree is green? And how is my brother?"

Why did the young man's wife object when his sister said that she would miss her mango tree?

....

....

Explain why the young man's wife neglected the tree.

....

....

Which words in the story so far would you use in your own writing, and why?

....

....

Understanding poetry

Read this **poem** aloud.

The Rabbit

We are going to see the rabbit.
We are going to see the rabbit.
Which rabbit, people say?
Which rabbit, ask the children?
Which rabbit?
The only rabbit,
The only rabbit in England,
Sitting behind a barbed-wire fence
Under the floodlights, neon lights,
Sodium lights,
Nibbling grass
On the only patch of grass
In England, in England
(Except the grass by the hoardings
Which doesn't count.)
We are going to see the rabbit
And we must be there on time.

First we shall go by escalator,
Then we shall go by underground,
And then we shall go by motorway
And then by helicopterway,
And the last ten yards we shall have to go
On foot.

And now we are going
All the way to see the rabbit,
We are nearly there,
We are longing to see it,
And so is the crowd
Which is here in thousands
With mounted policemen
And big loudspeakers
And bands and banners,
And everyone has come a long way.
But soon we shall see it
Sitting and nibbling
The blades of grass
On the only patch of grass
In – but something has gone wrong!
Why is everyone so angry,
Why is everyone jostling
And slanging and complaining?

The rabbit has gone,
Yes, the rabbit has gone.
He has actually burrowed down into the
    earth
And made himself a warren, under the earth,
Despite all these people.
And what shall we do?
What *can* we do?

It is all a pity, you must be disappointed,
Go home and do something else for today,
Go home again, go home for today.
For you cannot hear the rabbit, under the earth,
Remarking rather sadly to himself, by himself,
As he rests in his warren, under the earth:
'It won't be long, they are bound to come,
They are bound to come and find me, even here.'

Alan Brownjohn

Reading and understanding

Reread the **poem** on page 32, then answer the following questions in full sentences.

Is this **poem** about the past, the present or the future? What evidence is there in the poem for your answer?

....

....

Why do you think that this is the only rabbit on the only patch of grass?

....

....

What is a hoarding? D

....

....

Five ways of travelling are mentioned in the **poem**. What are they? Which is least harmful to the environment?

....

....

Find the **noun** that names the rabbit's home, then write another word for a rabbit's home. **Remember**: A **noun** is a naming word. D

....

Can you name the wild animals that live in a **sett**, an **earth** and a **holt**. D

....

....

Why is the rabbit sad?

....

....

In some places rabbits are regarded as pests. What does this mean?

....

....

Letter of complaint

Read this **letter**, then answer in full sentences the questions that follow.

Parkview,
Green Lane,
Greenford
11th April

The Chairman,
Greenford Council

Dear Sir,

I am writing to complain about the state of the waste ground, formerly known as Greenford Park, which can be seen from the front of my house.

I use the word "waste" deliberately as this, in truth, is what it has become.

Are we, as local residents, expected to suffer the misuse and probable ruination of this once useful, attractive amenity without expressing our feelings?

For the last month, I have noted the following thoughtless actions that have contributed to its present condition:

- the casual dropping of litter in the form of cans, fast-food packaging, etc.,
- the deliberate dumping of an old mattress,
- damage to the few remaining trees and wild plants from vehicles either crossing the area or parking on it,
- the careless behaviour of dog owners who allow their pets to foul the area without any attempt to clear up the mess that remains, thus endangering public health.

Added to these obvious forms of pollution, there is the noise from portable "music-making" devices in fine weather, which must contribute to the disappearance of the rabbits, badgers and other species from this once beautifully unspoilt wild area.

In these days of conservation and "green" awareness, I should have thought that our council might leap at the chance to create an area that would promote the preservation of plants and wildlife.

Yours faithfully,
Mr I. M. Wild

What is the writer's reason for writing? In which paragraph does he first state his reason?

....

....

Why does Mr Wild use inverted commas around the word "music-making"?

....

....

Reading and understanding

Answer the following questions about the **letter** on page 34.

How does the writer suggest that he is writing on behalf of everyone living in Greenford?

....

....

How does the writer make clear his four main complaints? What are they?

....

....

....

Why does Mr Wild use words such as **casual**, **deliberate**, **thoughtless** and **careless**?

....

....

The writer is trying to persuade the council to do something. Which words or phrases suggest this?

....

....

Is this just a **letter of complaint**, or does it make any suggestions for improvement? If so, what are they?

....

....

A **rhetorical question** is used to make people think, and an answer is not usually expected. Can you find the **rhetorical question** in this **letter** and write it here?

....

....

Do you think this letter will be successful? Why do you think this?

....

....

....

Reading a classic novel

In the nineteenth century, some writers wanted their readers to understand more about the lives of others. In those days before television and the Internet, books were one of the most important ways of **persuading** people to think about the rest of the world.

In Chapters 5 and 17 of his novel *Hard Times*, Charles Dickens describes Coketown, an industrial city in the north of England. Read his description of Coketown in these **extracts**.

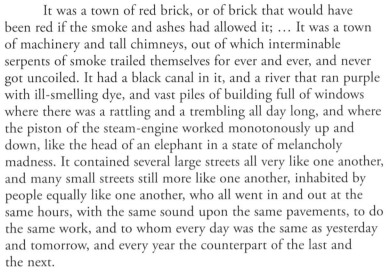

It was a town of red brick, or of brick that would have been red if the smoke and ashes had allowed it; … It was a town of machinery and tall chimneys, out of which interminable serpents of smoke trailed themselves for ever and ever, and never got uncoiled. It had a black canal in it, and a river that ran purple with ill-smelling dye, and vast piles of building full of windows where there was a rattling and a trembling all day long, and where the piston of the steam-engine worked monotonously up and down, like the head of an elephant in a state of melancholy madness. It contained several large streets all very like one another, and many small streets still more like one another, inhabited by people equally like one another, who all went in and out at the same hours, with the same sound upon the same pavements, to do the same work, and to whom every day was the same as yesterday and tomorrow, and every year the counterpart of the last and the next.

… The streets were hot and dusty on the summer day, and the sun was so bright that it even shone through the heavy vapour drooping over Coketown, and could not be looked at steadily. Stokers emerged from low underground doorways into factory yards, and sat on steps, and posts, and palings, wiping their swarthy visages, and contemplating coals. The whole town seemed to be frying in oil. There was a stifling smell of hot oil everywhere. The steam-engines shone with it, the dresses of the Hands were soiled with it, the mills throughout their many storeys oozed and trickled it … their inhabitants, wasting with heat, toiled languidly in the desert. But no temperature made the melancholy-mad elephants more mad or more sane. Their wearisome heads went up and down at the same rate in hot weather and cold, wet weather and dry, fair weather and foul. The measured motion of their shadows on the walls, was the substitute Coketown had to show for the shadows of rustling woods; while, for the summer hum of insects, it could offer, all the year round, from the dawn of Monday to the night of Saturday, the whirr of shafts and wheels.

Note: The extracts on pages 36 and 38 are being used to practise the reading skills, and may be harder than the actual SATs papers.

Reading and understanding

Answer these questions about the **extracts** on page 36.

Charles Dickens uses more detail than many modern writers would. Why do you think this is?

....

....

Dickens uses many long sentences and repeats words. What effect does this have on the reader?

....

....

Find as many **adjectives** describing **colours**, **sounds** and **smells** as you can.
Write them here.
Remember: An **adjective** is a describing word.

....

....

....

Find a **metaphor** for smoke and write it here.
Remember: A writer uses a **metaphor** to describe something as if it were something else.

....

Find a **simile** for a steam-engine and write it here.
Remember: A **simile** is used to compare one thing with another to create an image in the reader's mind. It often includes the words **like** or **as**.

....

Here are some of the words that you may have found unfamiliar or difficult. Draw a line to match each one with its meaning. The first one has been done for you. [D]

interminable	very sad
monotonously	leaked slowly
melancholy	endless
counterpart	weakly
wearisome	same
stokers	in the same dull way
visage	furnace feeders
oozed	boring and tiring
languidly	face

Reading another classic novel

Charles Dickens also wrote *David Copperfield*, a novel about a man's life. As a young boy, David is treated harshly by his stepfather and bullied at school. At the age of ten, he is sent to London to work. Being clever and ambitious, he finds the work very boring. Here, the grown-up David Copperfield describes that particular period in his life.

... I became, at ten years old, a little labouring hind in the service of Murdstone and Grinby.

Murdstone and Grinby's warehouse was at the water side. It was down in Blackfriars … it was the last house at the bottom of a narrow street, curving down hill to the river, with some stairs at the end, where people took boats. It was a crazy old house with a wharf of its own, abutting on the water when the tide was in, and on the mud when the tide was out, and literally over-run with rats. Its panelled rooms, discoloured with the dirt and smoke of a hundred years, I dare say; its decaying floors and staircase, the squeaking and scuffling of the old grey rats down in the cellars; and the dirt and rottenness of the place; are things, not of many years ago, in my mind, but of the present instant. They are all before me, just as they were in the evil hour when I went among them for the first time. …

Murdstone and Grinby's trade was among a good many kinds of people, but an important branch of it was the supply of wines and spirits to certain packet ships. … I think there were some among them that made voyages both to the East and West Indies. I know that a great many empty bottles were one of the consequences of this traffic, and that certain men and boys were employed to examine them against the light, and reject those that were flawed, and to rinse and wash them. When the empty bottles ran short, there were labels to be pasted on full ones, or corks to be fitted to them, or seals to be put upon the corks, or finished bottles to be packed in casks. All this work was my work, and of the boys employed upon it I was one.

Name the **narrator** of this part of the story. D

....

Explain the difference between a **narrator** and an **author**. D

....

....

....

Reading and understanding

Answer these questions about the **extract** on page 38.

The third **paragraph** describes the kind of work that the men and boys did.
Can you explain briefly what it was?

....

....

Can you complete these **old words** and **phrases** from the extract? They match the
meanings of the **modern words** given below. D

Modern word	Old word
next to	ab __ __ __ __ __ __ g
rotting	d __ __ __ __ __ __ __ g
now	of the p __ __ __ __ __ __ __ i __ __ __ __ __ __ t
journeys	vo __ __ __ __ s
a lot of	a gr __ __ t m __ __ y
results	co __ __ __ __ __ __ __ __ __ s
damaged	f __ __ __ __ d
put on	put __ __ __ __

A **hind** was a servant who lived in a house belonging to the master or mistress. Why is this
word used in the first sentence?

....

....

Do you think this **description** gives the reader a good idea of the way David felt? What
words can you think of to describe his feelings about his life and work at this time?

....

....

Fast fact-finding

Read the passage below.

Sky Colours

HAVE YOU EVER WONDERED why clear skies are sometimes deep blue and at other times almost white? Or why some sunsets are fiery red and others watery yellow? The reason is that the mixture of particles in the atmosphere is constantly changing. Every colour in the sky comes from the Sun. Sunlight is white, which means it is a mix of every colour in the rainbow. But as it passes through the atmosphere, gases, dust, ice crystals and water droplets split it into the various colours, bouncing some towards our eyes and absorbing others. The colours we see depend on which colours are reflected and which are absorbed. Clear skies are blue because gases in the air reflect mostly blue light from the Sun. The sky gets paler when extra dust or moisture reflects other colours, diluting the blue. Sunsets are yellow (or red, if the air is dusty) because the Sun's rays have to travel so far through the lower atmosphere that all the yellow light is absorbed.

From *How the Earth Works* by John Farndon

Underline all the **main points** in the paragraph above. Then answer these questions in full sentences.

What colour is sunlight?

....

Why is the sky blue?

....

....

What do you notice about the first four words? Why do you think they are set out this way?

....

....

What kind of sentences introduce the passage?

....

....

Words such as **the reason is**, **because** and **which means** tell us that this piece of writing does more than simply list facts. What else does it do?

....

....

Following instructions

Read the following piece of writing.

Experiment: Red and Blue Skies

It is not always easy to believe that all the colours in the sky come from the different way particles in the atmosphere reflect and absorb sunlight. But you can demonstrate it for yourself with this very simple experiment. The effects are quite subtle, and not always easy to see, so you need to conduct the experiment in a very dark room. Fill a straight glass with cold water, then add half a teaspoonful of milk. Now try shining the torch at the glass from different angles and watch how the colour of the milky water changes very slightly. Hold the torch close to the glass for a better effect. Add another half-teaspoonful of milk and repeat. Finally, add a full teaspoonful of milk, and try shining the torch at the glass from a variety of different angles.

From *How the Earth Works* by John Farndon

Read through the text again, underlining the actual **instructions**. On a separate sheet of paper, draw a **flow chart** that shows the **instructions** in the correct order.

Try the **experiment** yourself, then make **notes** under these headings.

Equipment/materials needed ....

....

What I did ....

....

....

What I saw ....

....

What I learnt from the experiment ....

....

....

Non-fiction writing

Non-fiction writing is based on facts and is different from stories, which come from an author's imagination. The following are all types of non-fiction writing: a retelling of real-life events; instructions; a technical explanation; an opinion or argument; a discussion; and a description of the characteristics of something. The chapters of non-fiction books can often be read in any order. Such books usually have a contents page, a glossary and an index.

Read this extract about the duck-billed platypus. Use the information to create an information leaflet. Give your piece of writing a heading and, if you want, use bullet points to highlight the animal's key characteristics.

All animals are different, but platypuses are particularly unusual animals. They look like a mixture of many other animals. They have flat tails, like beavers. They have thick fur that is well suited to water, like otters. They have bills and webbed feet, like ducks. Their webbed feet have claws, so they are able to dig and swim. Platypuses are also unusual because they are venomous mammals. A male platypus can sting other creatures to defend himself. Finally, platypuses are one of the very few mammals that lay eggs.

Onomatopoeia

FACTS

Onomatopoeia is the formation of words that imitate the sound of the objects or actions to which they refer. For example: **crunch**, **hiccup**, **ha-ha**, **vroom** and animal noises, such as **moo**, **miaow** and **oink**, are all onomatopoeic words. It is a form of figurative language, like personification.

Read this poem. In the space provided below, list the onomatopoeic words the poet has used in the poem.

Clocks

Ding, Dong, Ding, Dong!
The grandfather clocks aren't wrong.
The clocks' hands turn around,
Standing tall above the ground.
Ding, Dong, Ding, Dong!

Beep, Beep, Beep, Beep!
Says the stopwatch after his sleep.
He will stop at your every word.
That beep is what everyone heard.
Beep, Beep, Beep, Beep!

Bong, Bong, Bong, Bong!
Big Ben sounds like a gong.
Towering tall over London city,
Making citizens look so tiny.
Bong, Bong, Bong, Bong!

Tick, Tick, Tick, Tick!
Chimes the ongoing wall clock.
It will stay ticking forever.
When will it stop? Never!

Craig Robson (age 11)

....

....

....

Spelling, punctuation and grammar

SPaG tests

SPAG IS AN ACRONYM FOR **S**PELLING, **P**UNCTUATION, **A**ND **G**RAMMAR.

The two SPaG papers assess children's ability to spell, and their knowledge about grammar and punctuation. Formal grammar teaching was introduced with the new National Curriculum for English in 2014. The aim was to improve standards in writing and the understanding of the written word.

Spelling test

This test lasts about 15 minutes. The teacher reads out 20 short sentences, which are provided on the test paper but with certain words missing. Children have to fill in the missing words, spelling them correctly.

▽ All the words in the spelling paper will apply spelling rules in some way or have appeared on the statutory lists of spellings for upper and lower Key Stage 2.

REAL WORLD

Phonics and spelling patterns

Since starting school, children will have been taught spelling through learning phonics, the relationship between sounds and letters. The curriculum also aims to develop their understanding of word and spelling structure, and their knowledge of the rules for the most common spelling patterns, with some exceptions as well. New words appear in English all the time, largely due to rapidly changing technology. Many of these new words use existing parts of words such as the prefix cyber- for words *cyberspace* and *cybercafé*.

It is ___*likely*___ that it will rain tomorrow.

◁ **likely** tests the use of the "ly" suffix.

The dog ___*disobeyed*___ its owner.

◁ **disobeyed** tests the ability to add suffixes to words of more than one syllable.

The drum is part of the ___*percussion*___ family.

◁ **percussion** tests the different spelling of the /tion/ sound.

The prickly jumper was made from a ___*coarse*___ material.

◁ **coarse** tests the use of homophones.

SPaG test

This 45-minute assessment has 50 questions, which each carry one mark. Many of the questions ask children to pick the correct answer from a selection given.

Effective composition

involves forming, articulating, and communicating ideas, and then organising them coherently for a reader.

The National Curriculum, 2013

Which sentence is punctuated correctly?

Abdul called out, "will you come and help me?"

Abdul called out "will you come and help me"

Abdul called out, "will you come and help me"?

Abdul called out, "Will you come and help me?"

▷ The answer is sentence 4.

◁ A line or a box follows some questions, and children need to write a word, phrase, or short sentence.

Replace the underlined word or words in the sentence below with the correct **pronouns**.

For his ninth birthday, James visited his grandparents and <u>his grandparents</u> took <u>James</u> to the cinema.

◁ The answer is "they" and "him".

▷ The test starts with easier questions and moves on through to harder and more complex aspects of grammar. The grammatical terms are explained in a glossary in the National Curriculum, which can be accessed on the Department of Education website.

Which underlined group of words is a subordinate clause?

If you want to, <u>you can walk with us.</u>

This is the best fishing spot <u>we have found.</u>

We change places <u>when the bell rings.</u>

We planted the parsley next to the mint.

▷ The answer is sentence 3.

Preparing for the SPaG tests

CHILDREN NEED TO GO INTO THE TESTS
FEELING CONFIDENT.

The teaching of spelling, grammar, and punctuation
in schools can be supported by some fun and interesting
discussions at home. This shared time will also encourage
children to see the value of knowing how to spell, and
how to use grammar and punctuation as tools for improving
their writing.

Intrepid explorer

Terrifying tempest

Fun and useful

Encourage your child to see
learning spelling as fun and
useful. Correct spelling allows
other people to read and
understand what he or she
has written. Without any idea
of how to spell a word, a
dictionary is hard to use and a
spell checker may not
recognise the word wanted.

◁ Spell checkers also do
not recognise typing
mistakes or mistakes with
homophones – words
that sound the same but
are spelt differently.

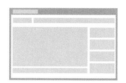

◁ Neither a dictionary nor
a machine can provide a
much better and more
exciting word that could
be used for improving a
piece of writing.

Interesting

Words in English are spelt in different
ways because of their origins, such as
Greek, Latin, or Old English. Word families
show how letter sounds have more than
one letter pattern. Knowing word origins
and word families can help children spell
unfamiliar words if they know the
spelling of a similar word.

▷ If you know how to spell
numeracy, then you can spell
numerical, because the word also
has something to do with
numbers, and is not spelt
newmerical or pneumerical.

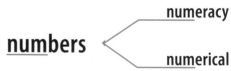

numeracy

numbers

numerical

▽ Collect and display
word families at home. This
is one for the /ai/sound.

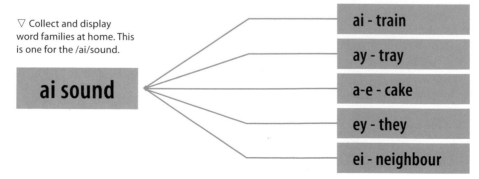

ai sound

ai - train

ay - tray

a-e - cake

ey - they

ei - neighbour

Reading

Unless children have a particular difficulty such as dyslexia, reading is a vital part of learning to spell. Just being exposed to spelling by reading the same word many times enables children to recognise when the word has been misspelt. In a test, your child can then identify any words spelt incorrectly and have another try at spelling them.

Encourage your child to read anything that she or he is interested in.

Spelling techniques

Not everyone learns to spell in the same way. Children are taught phonics first and then other spelling techniques. These spelling techniques help children to practise independently. They might turn a word into a picture, move the letters around in a word to make new words, or look, cover, and write a word.

Turn to pages 106 to 119 for some helpful spelling techniques.

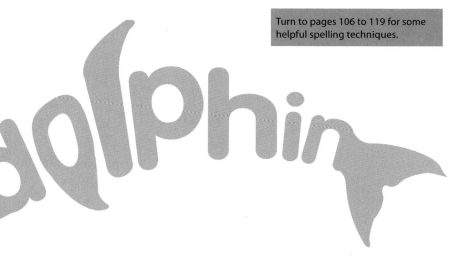

Word art for the spelling of dolphin

Explaining

Although some grammar may be unfamiliar to parents, children will have been taught the terms throughout their time at school. If uncertain, this is a great opportunity to ask your child to explain them to you. Your child can use their own writing to discuss how and why they wrote a particular sentence, which parts of speech and punctuation were used, and how the writing may be improved with interesting words and grammar.

Turn to pages 50 to 105 for explanations of some grammar and punctuation terms.

Proper nouns

A **proper noun** is the name of an actual person or place. A proper noun always begins with a capital letter.

Some proper nouns are the names of people:

Emily   Jack

Cindy Adams

Some proper nouns are the names of countries, cities or towns:

France

New York City

The names of months and days of the week are also proper nouns:

We go on holiday in **August**.

We start school on **Monday**.

Abstract nouns

Abstract nouns are names for things you can't see, hear or touch.

health

hunger

Some abstract nouns are feelings:

happiness

disappointment

Some abstract nouns are ideas:

speed

fame

Pronouns

Sometimes we don't want to keep repeating the same noun over and over again. Instead, we can use a **pronoun** to replace the noun.

Freddie is a fast runner.

~~Freddie~~ **He** always wins.

One day I want to beat ~~Freddie~~ **him**.

My sister wants to be a vet.

She loves animals.

Mum bought **her** a kitten.

My little **brother's bike** is broken.

He is going to mend **it**.

Owls hunt when **they** are hungry.

Small animals try to get away from **them**.

I, **me** and **you** are also pronouns. We use them instead of using our own name or someone else's name.

Please can **I** have another biscuit?

Can **you** teach **me** how to skateboard?

Words like **nothing**, **everything**, **nobody** and **somebody** are also pronouns.

There's **nothing** in my case.

I want to invite **everybody** to my party.

Dear Aiden, Please come to my party.

Nobody answered the door.

Somebody has eaten the pizza.

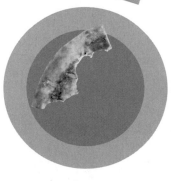

Top tip
When **I** is used as a pronoun, always write it as a capital letter.

Present and past tenses

Some things happen right now, in the present. Some things happened in the past. Different forms of a verb show when something happens. These are called **tenses**.

We use the **present tense** for things that happen now, every day, or every time. We use the **past tense** for things that happened in the past.

These are in the present:

It **snows** in winter.

We **plant** flowers each year.

These are in the past:

It **snowed** last night.

We **planted** some flowers last year.

With a lot of verbs, we add -**ed** at the end to make the past tense, but some verbs change completely.

This is in the present:

I always **win**.

This is in the past:

I **won** the race.

Future tense

No one really knows what will happen in the future, but we like talking about it. We can use **will** and **won't** (will not) if we feel sure about something in the future.

Of course I **will** win the race.

I definitely **won't** go to Mars.

We can use **might** or **may** if we're not so sure that something will happen.

The cat **might** catch the bird.

I **may** share my toys.

We can also say that we are **going to** do something in the future, if that's what we are planning to do.

I'm **going to** ride a bike.

I'm **going to** paint a a room.

Progressive tenses

We use different tenses to say whether something happens in the present, past or future. Sometimes we want to say that something isn't finished or it goes on for a long time. For this, we use the **progressive tense**.

We use the **present progressive** to say that something is happening right now.

He **is making** a sandcastle.

We **are skating** on the ice.

The dog **is burying** a bone.

The animals **are drinking**.

We use the normal present tense for things that happen every day or every week. However, we use the present progressive for something that is happening right now.

I **make** ← present something different every week.

Today, I **am making** a robot.
present progressive

We use the **past progressive** for things that kept happening for a while. We often use the past progressive to show that something else was happening at the same time.

I **was starting** to feel a bit sick!

The balloon **was going** higher and higher.

The fireworks **were making** a lot of noise.

I **was riding** my bike in the park, when a puppy ran out in front of me.

We use the past tense for things that happened and finished in the past. We use the past progressive for things that kept happening for a while.

The cat **climbed** to the top of the tree.

past

The cat **was climbing** up the tree.

past progressive

Top tip

The progressive form of a verb always ends in **-ing**.

Perfect tenses

The **perfect tenses** are two more tenses that we can use to talk about the past.

We use the **present perfect** when we are talking about something that happened in the past, but we are thinking about what it means **now**.

I have finished my homework!

The squirrel **has found** some nuts.

Look at the difference between the present perfect and the past tense:

I have lost my phone.

present perfect

I lost my phone, but my dad bought me a new one.

past

The dog **has gone** into the garden.

present perfect

The dog **went** into the garden and got very muddy!

past

In stories, we usually say what happened first, what happened next and what happened in the end. If we talk about something that happened earlier on, we use the **past perfect**.

We walked all day, and in the evening, we arrived at the gates of an old house. It was all quiet, and my companions wanted to go in. But my uncle **had warned** me that it was dangerous.

past perfect

This means my uncle warned me earlier, before we set out.

The professor opened the door to the laboratory and went in. He looked around, and listened carefully – nothing. With a feeling of horror, he realized that it was true. The dinosaurs **had escaped**!

past perfect

This means the dinosaurs escaped earlier, before the professor got to the laboratory.

Infinitives

The **infinitive** of a verb is the name of the verb, such as **eat**, **play** or **sleep**. It hasn't been changed to make different tenses. When you look up a verb in a dictionary, you look up the infinitive.

You can use the infinitive after **to**:

The witch decided **to make** a magic potion.

The monkey needs **to hold** on tight.

I don't want **to go** home!

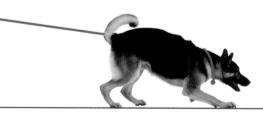

We set off **to explore** the forest.

Would you like **to stay** for lunch?

The bird is trying **to balance**.

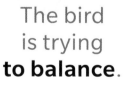

We also use the infinitive after verbs such as **can**, **will**, **might** and **must**. These verbs are called **modal verbs**.

I **can walk** on my hands.

I **might have** fish for dinner.

You **must pass** the ball.

You **should eat** plenty of fruit.

The spider hopes a fly **will come** along soon!

Don't worry, it **won't hurt**.

Adjectives

Adjectives tell us what people, animals and things are like. They describe nouns and tell you more about them. They might tell you what things look, sound or feel like.

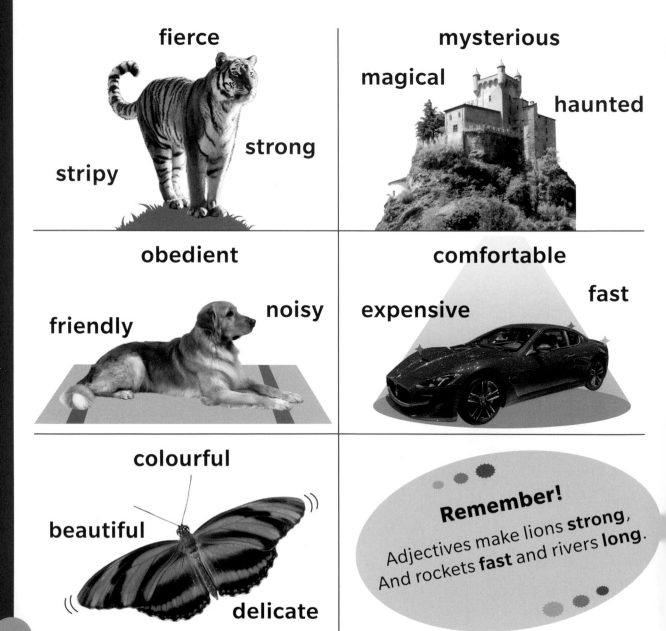

fierce

stripy

strong

mysterious

magical

haunted

obedient

friendly

noisy

comfortable

expensive

fast

colourful

beautiful

delicate

Remember!

Adjectives make lions **strong**, And rockets **fast** and rivers **long**.

Some adjectives describe the colour of something:

a **blue** and **yellow** hat with **red** pompoms

a **green** and **yellow** parrot

Some adjectives describe size or shape:

a **small** beetle with **big** jaws

a **triangular** piece of pizza on a **round** plate

Some adjectives describe feelings:

She's **content** and **relaxed**.

He's **happy** and **excited**.

Adverbs

Verbs tell you what things **do**. For example, tigers **roar** and birds **sing**. **Adverbs** tell you how they do it. Most adverbs end in **-ly**, and they usually come after verbs. Adverbs that tell you how someone does something are called **adverbs of manner**.

The lion roared **fiercely**.

Some birds can sing **beautifully**.

She tiptoed **quietly** down the stairs.

The sun was shining **brightly**.

I won **easily**.

You have to balance them **carefully**.

Top tip

Using adverbs to describe how people do things can make your writing more lively and interesting.

Some adverbs don't end in **-ly**, but they are still adverbs if they tell you how something is done.

I can run **fast**.

We played **well** today.

I always work **hard**.

You need to hold on **tight**.

Remember!

Without an adverb, you can smile,
Or ride a bike or sleep a while.
With adverbs, you smile **gleefully**,
Ride **skilfully**, sleep **peacefully**.

Comparatives and superlatives

Sometimes we might want to compare people or things to say how they are different. We use **comparatives** and **superlatives** to do this.

heavy   heavier   heaviest

expensive

more expensive

most expensive

We use comparatives to compare two people or things.

A train is **faster** than a bike.

A lion is **more dangerous** than a mouse.

We use superlatives to compare three or more people or things.

A plane is the **fastest**.

A tiger is the **most dangerous**.

With short adjectives, we add -**er** to make comparatives and -**est** to make superlatives.

A camel is **slower** than a gazelle.

A tortoise is the **slowest**.

With longer adjectives, we use **more** to make comparatives and **most** to make superlatives.

Ice-skating is **more difficult** than riding a scooter.

Walking on a tightrope is the **most difficult**.

The adjectives **good** and **bad** have irregular comparatives and superlatives. This means they take different forms.

★ a **good** mark

★ ★ a **better** mark

★ ★ ★ the **best** mark you can get

My sister's socks smell really **bad**.

My dad's socks smell even **worse**.

My brother's socks smell the **worst** of all!

Prepositions

We use **prepositions** to show how different nouns relate to each other in a sentence. Prepositions are small words, such as **on**, **in**, **to** and **with**.

See how prepositions link the nouns and pronouns in these sentences:

dog ball garden	I castle secret passage

The dog is playing **with** a ball **in** the garden.	I got **into** the castle **through** a secret passage.
astronaut Moon rocket	Mum cake me birthday

The astronaut flew **to** the Moon **in** a rocket.	Mum made a cake **for** me **on** my birthday.

Prepositions of place

Some prepositions tell us **where** something is or which direction it goes in.

The rabbit is **in** the basket.

The books are **on** the table.

He's diving **under** the water.

Can you find your way **through** the maze?

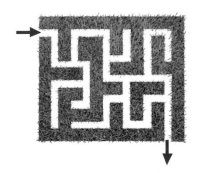

The horse jumped **over** the fence.

The squirrel is running **along** the branch.

Coordinating conjunctions

The conjunctions **and**, **but** and **or** are called **coordinating conjunctions** because they link words, phrases and clauses that are equally important.

I got 10 out of 10 in a test **and** I got a star!

Whales live in the oceans **and** they mainly eat fish.

I like tennis, **but** my brother prefers football.

I wanted a kitten, **but** my mum said no!

Shall we play a video game **or** go to the park?

Would you like an apple **or** a banana?

Subordinating conjunctions

Conjunctions that **aren't** coordinating conjunctions are called **subordinating conjunctions**. They link a subordinate (less important) clause to a main clause. The subordinate clause often gives a reason for something, says when something happens or gives extra information.

You can't go on that ride **because** you're too small.

Tigers only hunt **when** they are hungry.

We've been friends **since** we were three.

You can have some pizza **if** you're hungry.

I felt excited **as** I opened the door.

I love Barney, **although** he is very grumpy-looking!

Interjections

An **interjection** is a single word that expresses a thought or feeling. You often shout or say interjections loudly, and so they are often followed by an exclamation mark.

Hello! We're over here.

Bye! See you later!

Thanks! Can I open it now?

Congratulations! You won!

Shh! Don't make any noise.

Wow! What a strange-looking animal. What is it?

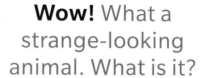

(It's a Malayan tapir!)

We often use interjections to show how we are feeling.

Brrr!
I'm cold.

Hooray!
It's sports day.

Ugh!
A spider!

Hey! That's my ball! Give it back!

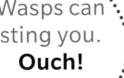

Wasps can sting you.
Ouch!

Oops!
It broke.

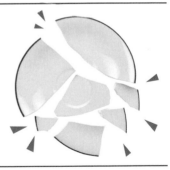

Remember!

Hi! Hello!
If you want my attention ...
Wow! Hooray!
Use an interjection!

Determiners

Nouns are words for things, animals and people. **Determiners** are words that go before nouns. They tell you which thing or person you are talking about.

The words **a**, **an** and **the** are determiners. They are also sometimes called articles.

It's **a** horse.

Look at **the** penguins!

The words **this**, **that**, **these** and **those** are also determiners.

This ice lolly is delicious!

Look at **those** fish!

Numbers are determiners, too:

I've got **six** pencils.

There are **five** puppies.

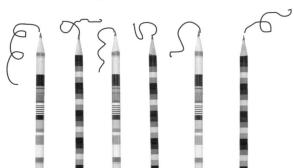

Words like **some**, **any** and **many** are determiners. We use them to talk about amounts of things, but without saying exactly how many there are.

There are **some** tadpoles in the pond.

There aren't **many** clouds in the sky.

Some determiners tell us who something belongs to. These are called possessive determiners. The possessive determiners are: **my**, **your**, **his**, **her**, **its**, **our**, **their**.

My hair is getting quite long.

Their sandcastle is amazing!

Adjectives can come before nouns, to describe them. Determiners always come before adjectives.

Look at **that little** pony!

determiner ↗   adjective ↖

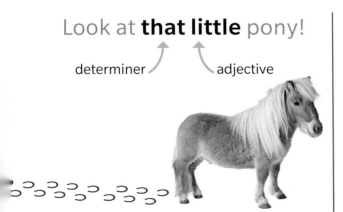

Do you like **my new** shoes?

determiner ↗   adjective ↖

Statements

A **statement** is a sentence that gives us information or tells part of a story. It starts with a capital letter and ends with a full stop.

These statements give us information.

Giant pandas eat bamboo.

Pumpkins are tasty, and you can also use them to make lanterns.

These statements tell part of a story.

The king invited us into the castle for a feast.

Dan looked at the treasure map excitedly.

You can also end a statement with an exclamation mark (!), to make it sound more exciting.

I scored three goals today!

We ran back to the helicopter, but the engine wouldn't start!

Questions

A **question** is a sentence that asks something. It starts with a capital letter and ends with a question mark (?).

Is that your guinea pig?

Do you like oranges?

We often use words like **who**, **what**, **which**, **where**, **why**, **how**, **when** and **whose** in questions.

What have you got in your lunch box?

Who wants to play basketball with me?

Why are your shoes so dirty?

Where do polar bears live?

Top tip You can use questions when you are writing a story, to create a feeling of mystery. For example, **I picked up the old box. What was inside it?**

Exclamations

An **exclamation** is a sentence that begins with **What** or **How**. It expresses a strong feeling of happiness, surprise, anger or fear. It starts with a capital letter and ends with an exclamation mark.

What beautiful flowers!

What big claws it's got!

What an amazing cave!

How scary!

How cute they are!

How delicious that meal looks!

Top tip
You can also use an exclamation mark at the end of a statement to make it sound more exciting. For example, **We drove really fast!** This is still a statement, not an exclamation, because exclamations always begin with **What** or **How**.

Commands

A **command** is a sentence that tells someone to do something. It starts with a capital letter and can end with a full stop or an exclamation mark.

Some commands are instructions.

Mix the flour and the butter.

Glue the patterned paper onto your picture.

We use an exclamation mark when someone says a command loudly or gives an order.

Be careful!

Sit!

Slow down!

Don't eat all our nuts!

Noun phrases

Nouns are the names of things, animals and people, such as **tree**, **tiger** and **brother**. A **noun phrase** is a group of words that all belong with the noun and tell us more about it.

Look at how we can add words to the noun **dog** to make a noun phrase that describes what the dog is like.

a small dog

a small white dog with a little orange collar

a small white dog with a little orange collar and a flowing cape

A noun phrase is not a sentence. It doesn't begin with a capital letter and end with a full stop. It just gives more information about a noun. In a sentence, we can use a noun phrase like a noun.

We saw a ship.

We saw **an old sailing ship with three tall masts**.

Top tip

Using longer noun phrases can make your writing more interesting.

Prepositional phrases

Prepositions are words such as **on**, **in**, **to** and **with**.
Prepositions are always followed by a noun or pronoun.
A **prepositional phrase** is the preposition and the
following noun or pronoun together.

There are some fish
in the water.

She slid **down the slide**.

The cat
jumped **onto
my lap**.

I like pizza
**with cheese
and tomato**.

I got a new toy
**for my
birthday**.

I went to
bed **at eleven
o'clock**!

Adverbials

Adverbials do the same job as adverbs. They describe **how**, **why**, **when** or **where** something happens. While adverbs are always one word, adverbials can be one word or several words.

These adverbials tell us **how** something happens:

The rabbit appeared **magically**.

It appeared **as if by magic**.

He fought **bravely**.

He fought **with great courage**.

These adverbials tell us **where** or **when** something happens:

Kitty's hiding **over there**.

She's hiding **behind the bag**.

It's my birthday **tomorrow**.

It's my birthday **on the tenth of July**.

Top tip

Adverbials answer these questions:
How? **When**? **Why**? **Where**?

Fronted adverbials

Adverbials often come at the end of a sentence. However, you can put them at the beginning of a sentence if they're important and you want them to stand out. These are called **fronted adverbials**.

Once upon a time, there was a lion cub called Larry.

Every weekday, we go to school on the bus.

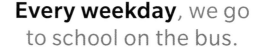

Slowly and cautiously, Tabitha opened the door and went inside.

As quickly as I could, I put on my spacesuit and got ready for my spacewalk.

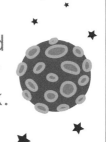

Finally, it was time to open my presents!

Actually, it's a koala, not a bear!

Clauses

Verbs are words that tell you what someone or something does, such as **sing**, **go** and **play**. A **clause** is a group of words that contains a verb.

we play indoors

it's snowing

he is happy

I'm going on holiday

Some clauses can also be a sentence on their own, if you give them a capital letter and a full stop.

We're happy.

It's snowing!

You can put clauses together to make longer sentences. To do this, you add a word to join the two clauses together. You join clauses together with **conjunctions**.

We play indoors **when** it's snowing.

He is happy **because** he's going on holiday.

There are different ways to join clauses together in a sentence.

the magician waved his wand + the prince turned into a frog

The magician waved his wand **and** the prince turned into a frog.

The prince turned into a frog **as soon as** the magician waved his wand.

kangaroos can jump far + they have powerful back legs

Kangaroos can jump far **because** they have powerful back legs.

Kangaroos have powerful back legs **so** they can jump far.

Main clauses

A **main clause** is a clause that makes sense on its own, so it also works as a sentence on its own. All sentences must have at least one main clause.

I got a kite for my birthday, so I went to the park.

This is a main clause because it could be a sentence on its own.

This is not a main clause because it doesn't make sense on its own.

I was terrified when I saw the spider.

The main clause doesn't have to come first in the sentence.

As soon as it was dark, **the badger set off to find food**.

This is not a main clause.

This is a main clause.

Because it was hot, **we stayed in the shade**.

This is not a main clause.

This is a main clause.

Top tip

If a clause is a main clause, you can make it into a sentence on its own.

We use conjunctions to link clauses together. The conjunctions **and**, **but** and **or** are called coordinating conjunctions. When we use these conjunctions to join clauses, we say that both clauses are main clauses. In these sentences, both the underlined clauses are main clauses.

It's raining and I'm happy!

I like tennis and I like basketball.

We opened the chest, but it was empty.

I read a book, but then I lost it.

Meerkats eat insects or they sometimes eat snakes' eggs.

We can play the guitar or we can bang on the drums.

Subordinate clauses

A clause that doesn't make sense on its own is called a **subordinate clause**. Subordinate clauses often begin with conjunctions such as **after**, **before**, **because**, **as**, **when**, **while**, **if**, **since** and **although**. These conjunctions are called **subordinating conjunctions**.

I was amazed **when I saw all the presents**.

We'll be late for school **if we don't hurry**!

Charley's excited **because it's time for his walk**.

I always clean my teeth **before I go to bed**.

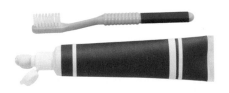

Sometimes a subordinate clause can come first in a sentence.

Although they are small, bees do a very important job.

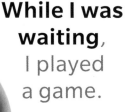

While I was waiting, I played a game.

Relative clauses

Sometimes you might want to add more information about someone or something that you are talking about. To join this extra information into one sentence, you can use a **relative clause**. Relative clauses often begin with **who**, **which** or **that**.

astronauts are people + they go into space

Astronauts are people **who go into space**.

scientists often use microscopes + they make tiny things look bigger

Scientists often use microscopes, **which make tiny things look bigger**.

dinosaurs were huge creatures + they lived millions of years ago

Dinosaurs were huge creatures **that lived millions of years ago**.

You can also use a relative clause to make a comment about a whole idea and give your opinion.

I'm going to be in a play, **which is exciting**!

Relative pronouns

Relative pronouns are words such as **who**, **which**, **that**, **where** and **when**. We use them in relative clauses to add more information about a person or thing.

We use **who** to add more information about people, and we use **which** to add more information about things.

A magician is a person **who** does magic tricks.

Rhinos live in Africa, **which** is a big continent.

We can use **that** for either people or things.

The player **that** gets the most counters into the hole is the winner.

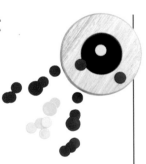

I'm playing on the swing **that** I got for my birthday.

We use **where** to give more information about a place, and **when** to give more information about a time.

Small birds try to find a safe place **where** they can nest.

I can remember the day **when** I started school.

We use **whose** to say who something belongs to.

I played
with Dan,
whose new
trampoline
is amazing!

It's Dan's trampoline –
it belongs to him.

This is Elsie,
whose cat
follows her
everywhere.

It's Elsie's cat –
it belongs to her.

We can sometimes leave out the relative pronouns **who**, **which** and
that. We can leave them out when the person or thing we are talking
about is the object of a verb. Compare these sentences:

Parrots are birds
that can learn
to talk.

Hello

Parrots are birds
~~that~~ you can
teach to talk.

Parrots are the subject
because they can learn to talk.
We can't leave out "that".

Parrots are the object because
we teach them to talk.
We can leave out "that".

We sometimes use **whom** in formal writing. We use it when the person we
are talking about is the object of a verb. Compare these two sentences:

Here, Max is
the subject.

Max is the one **who** loves me true.

Here, Max is
the object.

Max is the one **whom** I love too!

Top
tip

We can never leave out the relative
pronouns **where**, **when** or **whose**.

Active and passive sentences

In **active sentences**, the **doer** of the action comes first.
In **passive sentences**, you can change the order around,
and put the **receiver** of the action first.

This is an active sentence:

Noah caught the ball.

This is a passive sentence:

The ball was caught
by Noah.

Notice that we change the verb in passive sentences.

My sister
made these
cakes.

These cakes
were made
by my
sister.

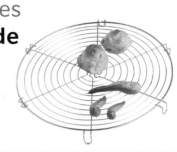

Remember!
Active and passive are simple, you see:
If I hit the ball, the ball is hit by me!

We often use passive sentences when we don't know who did the action of the verb.

Some jewels **were stolen** from the castle last night.

My jumper **was made** in America.

We also use the passive if we want to focus on what happened, rather than on who did something.

My boots **have been cleaned**!

Her fur **has been clipped**.

In passive sentences we can add the doer of the action, using **by**.

These paw prints were made **by a dog**.

The first practical telephone was invented **by Alexander Graham Bell**.

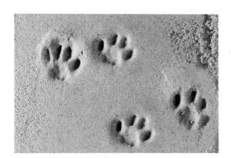

Direct speech

In stories, we often write about what people say to each other. When we write **direct speech**, we write exactly what someone says, and we use inverted commas (speech marks).

"Let's go and find the treasure."

"Look, there's a rainbow!"

 "Is there anyone in there?"

 "Go away!"

"There's a shark in the water!"

"It's a secret."

Top tip When you use direct speech in your writing, try using lots of different verbs instead of just **said**. Try verbs such as **cried**, **shouted**, **whispered** and **screamed**.

Reported speech

When we use **reported speech**, we report back what the person said. We don't give their exact words, and we don't use inverted commas (speech marks).

This is direct speech:

"I'm cold."

This is reported speech:

Beth said that she was cold.

"What's in your bag?"

Molly asked me what was in my bag.

"The bouncy castle is amazing!"

Anthony said that the bouncy castle was amazing.

"Where has the hamster gone?"

Oliver asked where the hamster had gone.

Capital letters

Sentences always begin with a **capital letter**. So a capital letter shows you where a new sentence starts.

We had our sports day last week. **I**t was fun. **E**veryone enjoyed it.

We use capital letters for the names of people and places.

Meet my brother **J**oe and my sister **A**lice. We were born in **N**ew **Y**ork **C**ity in the **USA**, but we now live in **S**ydney, **A**ustralia.

We use capital letters in the titles of books and films, but not for every word.

I'm reading *Charlie and the Chocolate Factory*.

The names of days of the week and months always start with a capital letter, too.

My birthday is on 12th **S**eptember. This year, it's on a **S**aturday.

September						
S	M	T	W	T	F	S
			1	2	3	4	5
6	7	8	9	10	11	12
13	14	15	16	17	18	19
20	21	22	23	24	25	26
27	28	29	30			

Always use a capital letter when you use the word **I** to talk about yourself.

I climbed into the canoe and **I** started to paddle down the river.

Full stops

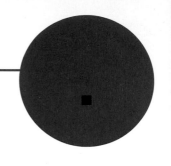

You use a **full stop** at the end of a sentence. It shows that the sentence is finished. Don't forget that after a full stop you need to use a capital letter to start your next sentence.

This is an African elephant.
It has a long trunk and big ears.
It eats grass, leaves and
other vegetation.

You can make really **long sentences** when you write stories by adding lots of exciting **adjectives** and **adverbs** to describe exactly what is happening, but in the end there always has to be a full **STOP**.

Sometimes a full stop can be used at the end of shortened, or abbreviated, words. But it is also acceptable not to include the full stop.

Dr. stands for "Doctor"

e.g. stands for "for example"

dept. stands for "department"

D.C., in Washington D.C., stands for "District of Columbia"

Question marks

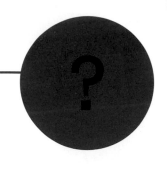

If you are writing a question, you need to put a **question mark** at the end of the sentence.

Can you ride a bike**?**

Who made these biscuits**?**

How many oranges are there**?**

Where is your rabbit**?**

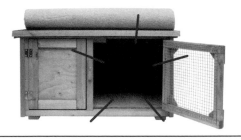

After a question mark, you need to use a capital letter to start your next sentence.

I looked at the old wooden chest. Who did it belong to**?** What was inside it**?** There was only one way to find out.

Exclamation marks

!

You can use an **exclamation mark** at the end of a sentence instead of a full stop. An exclamation mark makes a sentence sound more exciting. It suggests that someone is surprised, happy, angry or scared. It can also suggest that someone is shouting.

Go away!

What a scary dinosaur!

After an exclamation mark, you need to use a capital letter to start your next sentence.

We won the competition! We were the champions.

What a cute kitten! Can we take her home?

Top tip Try not to use exclamation marks all the time. If you use them occasionally they'll have more impact!

Commas

You use **commas** to separate different things in a list. You usually use **and** or **or** before the last thing in the list, and you don't usually use a comma before **and** or **or**.

The balloons are red, yellow, green and blue.

You can have an apple, an orange, a banana or some grapes.

You use commas between different clauses in a sentence. The comma separates the different ideas in the sentence and makes the sentence easier to understand.

I'm older than Joaquin, but he's taller than me.

Owls are nocturnal, so they come out at night.

You can also use commas to separate out part of a sentence that is extra information. Notice that you use a comma **before** and **after** the extra information.

Jake, who is in my class, is really good at roller-skating.

Young bears, which are born in the winter, have to learn to find food.

You use a comma before or after someone's name to show that someone is speaking to them.

Come here, Winston!

Mum, can I go on that ride?

You can use a comma to separate two adjectives before a noun.

She's got long, curly hair.

Peacocks have large, colourful tails.

When you start a sentence with an adverb or an adverbial, you use a comma after it, before you begin the main part of the sentence.

Luckily, I still had the magic ring.

Once upon a time, there was a beautiful princess.

Top tip When you use commas in direct speech, always put them inside the inverted commas.

Apostrophes

Sometimes you can join two words together into one word, such as **don't** (do not). These joined words don't include all the letters of both words. You use an **apostrophe** to replace the missing letters.

Guinea pigs
don't
eat meat.
do not

We've
got a new car.
we have

she is
She's a very
good dancer.

It **isn't** raining now.
is not

There are some contractions that we would not usually write as separate words. In the past, they were written separately, but today we use contractions.

Let's
play cards.
let us

The clock struck
twelve o'clock.

twelve of
the clock

Possessive apostrophes

You can use an apostrophe with an **-s** to show who something belongs to. This is called a **possessive apostrophe**. If you possess something, you own it.

You can use a possessive apostrophe after someone's name or after a noun.

These are Olivia**'s** shoes.

Those are my dad**'s** glasses.

If you are talking about more than one person or thing, and the noun you are using ends in **-s**, you just add the apostrophe. You don't add another **s**. Compare these sentences:

The chick**'s** feathers are yellow.

The chick**s'** feathers are yellow.

Some nouns end in -**ss** even when you are only talking about one person or thing, and some names end in -**s**. These words add **'s** as usual for possession.

Look at the princess**'s** beautiful dress.

James**'s** new train set is amazing!

Colons

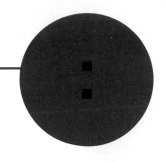

You use a **colon** to introduce a list. You can also use a colon to join two ideas together into one sentence.

You use a colon to introduce a list.

My favourite sports are: hockey, basketball and tennis.

To go camping, you need: a tent, a stove for cooking and a sleeping bag.

These are my friends: Ellie, Rohan and Sarah.

I've got three pets: a hamster, a guinea pig and a new kitten.

You can also use a colon to join two ideas together into one sentence. You use a colon when the second idea explains the first idea.

Lions are predators: they hunt and kill other animals for food.

This car is really fast: it can travel at 240 km (150 miles) per hour.

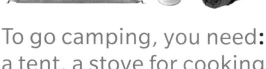

Top tip Never use a capital letter after a colon unless it's the first letter of a proper noun.

Semi-colons

You can use a **semi-colon** to join two ideas together into one sentence to show that the ideas are closely linked. Never use a capital letter after a semi-colon unless it's the first letter of a proper noun.

There are lots of monkeys in the safari park; there are elephants and giraffes, too.

I love flying my kite; it goes really high!

My uncle can make animals out of balloons; he's going to teach me how to do it.

I've never been on a plane before; I'm really excited!

You can also use semi-colons instead of commas to separate different things in a list. It's best to use semi-colons when each thing on the list is quite long and complicated.

To make your monster mask, you will need: a large piece of plain card; paints and brushes; a small pot of glitter; scissors and glue.

Sing a spelling

I am a noisy songbird! I know a trick that may help you learn your spellings: turn the rule or a particular spelling into a rhyme or mini song.

Music is a useful way to learn, and a rhyme or tune can help you remember. Sing a tune with me!

Good idea!

people

To the tune of Happy Birthday:

"p-e-o-p-l-e, p-e-o-p-l-e, p-e-o-p-l-e, that's how you spell people."

plural rule

Add a well-known tune to these words:
"For most plurals, just add an **s**,
that just means there is more than **one**,
but some plurals sound like /**ez**/
then you know you add **es**."

CAN YOU pick a rhyme you know well?

Make up a rhyme for spelling this word.

surprise

Start thinking!

Turn this rule into a different rhyme.

plural rule

107

Does it look right?

Spelling can be a very prickly job! The spelling of some words follows the rules, but for other words you just have to learn how to spell them. To help you learn, have a go at spelling the word and see if it looks right.

And for an extra prickly tip: if it looks wrong then have another go, maybe by using a different way of spelling the same sound.

Good idea!

porcupine

por is spelt just how it sounds, and **pine** follows the rules. But the middle bit sounds like /**q**/ – **porqpine**. This doesn't look right! There would never be a **q** next to a **p**. So either look the word up in a dictionary or have another go.

Follow these steps:

Step 1

What sounds can you hear when you say the word? How many sounds can you hear? Are there any sounds that have two letters or more?

Step 2

Have a go at spelling the word yourself and then see if it looks right.

Step 3

If it doesn't, try again, then check with an adult or in a dictionary.

CAN YOU try spelling the names of these animals, using the three steps?

Start thinking!

CAN YOU?

109

Hopping around letters

I am a grasshopper and I have a challenge for you! I just can't keep still, and neither can the letters in my name. The letters want to hop around and make new words of all different lengths.

How many different words can you make with the letters in 'grasshopper'?

Good idea!

Start off by working out the different digraphs you can use, for example **er**, **sh** and **oe**. Can you find any others? Put them as headings in the boxes. Then see how many different words you can make using the letters.

s h

shape
rash

e r

o e

g r a s s h o p p e r

It might help to cut the letters out on a piece of paper and move them around, or use a piece of paper to try out spellings and see if they look right.

Good idea!

111

An elephant never forgets

They say an elephant never forgets anything. **Mnemonics** is a very tricky word for a way of remembering some of the more complicated spellings.

A **mnemonic** uses each of the letters in a word to give you a reminder of the spelling.

Good idea!

because

big **e**lephants **c**an't **a**lways **u**se **s**mall **e**xits

rhythm

rhythm **h**as **y**our **t**wo **h**ips **m**oving

necessary

it is ne**ces**sary to have one **c**ollar but two **s**leeves

CAN YOU?

CAN YOU create a mnemonic for each of these words?
Will you still remember them in a few days' time?

guard

answer

occasion

How to remember the echidna

I am an echidna. I'm a very unusual type of creature that lives in Australia. You may never have heard of me before, and my name is certainly a very tricky word to spell. So here are some ideas that might help you remember my name.

Good idea!

Have a picture in your head of the word as well as the animal so that it sticks in your brain and looks familiar.

Write the word ten times.

echidna

echidna, echidna, echidna, echidna, echidna, echidna, echidna, echidna, echidna, echidna

Think! This animal looks a bit like a hedgehog.

Split up the word into pieces.

e-chid-na

Use phonics, although this word does not sound the same as it is spelt.

Turn the word into a picture.

echidna

It has tall letters in the middle and shorter ones either side.
Notice the word **hid** in the middle.

? **CAN YOU follow these three steps with these words?**

country

gardening

Watch out for the rat!

I am the rat in separate. Separate is one of the most commonly misspelled words. Even adults don't always know how to spell it!

Good idea!

To remember that it's an **/ar/** sound, not an **/er/** sound, in the middle of sep**arat**e, remember **a rat!**

Sound out the word.

s – e – p – ar – a-e – t

Find the word within.

sep-a-rat-e

Write the word ten times.

separate

separate, separate, separate, separate, separate,

separate, separate, separate, separate, separate

CAN YOU sound these words out and find the hidden word?

peculiar

business

disappoint

Word art

I am a dolphin and I love to **leap** and *twirl*. My name is tricky to spell as it has a **ph** and not an **f** in it.

Turn the word you are learning to spell into a picture to help you remember it.

Good idea!

dolphin

tremor

squirrel

SQUIRREL

CAN YOU turn these words into a picture?

bounce

rainbow

119

Silent consonants

FACTS

Some consonants are silent in the spelling of a word. They are written, but not pronounced. The secret silent consonants lurk where you cannot hear them. You will never know they are there, unless you know how to spell the word. For example: the **b** in **limb** and the **w** in **sword** are both silent consonants.

Look at the words in the word bank carefully. Then, fill in each silent-consonant box.

crumb	knee	doubt	wrist
dough	who	high	right
knuckle	knot	neighbour	lamb
write	wreck	knife	plumber

silent B

....
....
....
....

silent W

....
....
....
....

silent GH

....
....
....
....

silent K

....
....
....
....

120

Root words

A **root word** is usually a complete word in itself, such as **order** or **break**.
You can, however, make a new word by adding a prefix or a suffix to a root word.
For example: **dis** + **order** = **disorder** and **break** + **able** = **breakable**.

Remove the prefix or suffix from each of the words below to find the root word.

Word	Root word
misbehave	....
sincerely	....
training	....
semicircle	....
disagree	....
intensify	....
submarine	....
disappear	....
equipped	....
lengthen	....
drinkable	....
preschool	....

Now pick any two pairs of words from the chart above. Write four sentences, each
including one of the words you picked.

....

....

....

....

Prefixes

FACTS

A **prefix** is a group of letters added to the beginning of a root word to change its meaning. For example: **dis** + **approve** = **disapprove**.

Match each prefix to its meaning below. **Hint**: think about the words you know that use these prefixes and their meanings.

dis	again or back
de	reverses the meaning of the verb
mis	badly or wrongly
re	do the opposite of

Choose and write the correct prefix from the exercise above for each of these root words.

.............appear

...............arrange

...............frost

...............cycle

...............value

...............place

Suffixes

A **suffix** is a group of letters added to the end of a root word to change its meaning. For example: **walk** + **ing** = **walking**. Suffixes are not complete words and cannot be used on their own in a sentence.

Change the nouns and adjectives into verbs by adding one of these suffixes: **ate**, **ify**, **ise** or **en**.

Nouns/Adjectives	Verbs
standard	....
straight	....
note	....
elastic	....
deep	....
hyphen	....
apology	....
dead	....
pure	....
loose	....
glory	....

What do you notice about the root words above ending in **y** and **e**?

....

Choose two verbs from the exercise above and write sentences using them.

....

....

Antonyms

An **antonym** is a word that has an opposite meaning to another word.

For example:

forget means the opposite of **remember**

Write an antonym for each of these words.

strong	....
first	....
near	....
youngest	....
clean	....
good	....
question	....
dark	....

Now try these. Read each complete word and then fill in the missing letters of the word beside it to make an antonym.

shorten	len___en	vertical	horiz___al
hope	des___r	compulsory	volun___y
antonym	sy_____m	optional	nec___ary

Antonyms: using a prefix

FACTS

Antonyms are sometimes made by adding a prefix.

For example: **edible**   **inedible**

Choose from the prefixes **un**, **in** and **dis** to make each word mean the opposite.
Write the antonym in the space provided.

Word	Antonym
safe	....
expensive	....
willing	....
agree	....
complete	....
comfort	....

Complete these sentences using the correct antonym.
Hint: look at the words in italics and use the prefixes you have just learned.

The instructor was clearly not *qualified* to teach the class;
therefore, he was ....

At first the magician's assistant was *visible* and then after he
said the magic words she was   ....!

I *like* to munch on apples, but I have a strong
.....................................for apple pie.

Punctuation: getting it right!

FACTS

There are lots of different types of punctuation, but it is very important to use the correct punctuation in the correct places. Otherwise, the meaning of a sentence may not be clear and will confuse the reader.

Eloise sometimes forgets to use the correct punctuation in her writing. Read her sentences and add the corrections where necessary. Use the key below to add missing punctuation marks. Where a small letter needs to be capital, add a star (*) next to it.

" "	inverted commas/speech marks
.	full stop
,	comma

I want to go to the beach! shouted Chloe

is that a clown? asked Freya

it was time to go It had been a hard day

I think that is hilarious laughed Leon

That really hurt! yelled leah

it has all been worth it

daniel bought oranges apples bread and milk

I am going on holiday soon

Now write a sentence demonstrating the use of each type of punctuation.

....

....

Advanced punctuation

Properly punctuated written English ensures that sentences can be understood clearly and avoids ambiguity, or double meaning.

Match each of the punctuation marks first to its name and then to its definition.

;	apostrophe	This mark sometimes links two or more simple sentences that share a common theme.
:	hyphen	This mark is used to show that an example, explanation or list is to follow.
-	colon	This mark is used to link words or parts of words.
,	semi-colon	This mark is used to show possession or a contraction.

Now read the sentences below carefully and fill in the correct punctuation marks.
Hint: you can also use other punctuation marks that you have already learned.

There s a reason why I didn t go to Adam s party
I didn t have a fancy dress costume

Is this café self service

Its a really exciting day today you can tell its her birthday

Is this book yours   the teacher asked
No its Zoe s I replied

Isobel had an X ray of her arm

Don t do that

Colons and semi-colons in lists

Punctuation can be quite complicated and confusing. It is helpful to read written work aloud to help you decide where the punctuation marks should go.

A **colon** (:) is used before a list of words, phrases or clauses. Here is an example. The following werc in the boot of the car: beach balls, buckets and spades.

A **semi-colon** (;) is used in a list to separate items that are longer than one or two words. Here is an example. There were several new features in the garden: a pond; a sensory trail along the path; a willow dome; and a bench area for picnics. **Note**: unlike commas, a semi-colon is used before the final item in the list.

Look at the items in the boot of the car below. Write a sentence using a colon to punctuate the list of the items you see.

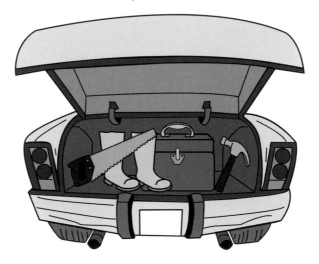

....

....

Read the sentence below. It lists a number of items you might find in a garden. Add semi-colons in the right places to separate the items in the list. **Remember**: semi-colons are used to separate items that are longer than one or two words.

These are the items in my shed: a spade to dig the soil a watering can to water the plants a pair of gloves and a set of ceramic flower pots.

Colons and semi-colons in lists

Colons and semi-colons are also used in bulleted lists. A colon is used before the list begins and semi-colons are used to separate the various items. A full stop is used at the end of the list because it is also the end of the sentence.
Here is an example.

Equipment required for PE:
- shorts;
- T-shirt;
- trainers.

Think of all the things you might need to pack if you were going away on holiday.
Then make a list of the items using a colon and semi-colons.

....

- ....

- ....

- ....

- ....

- ....

- ....

Next time you need to make a list, punctuate it with colons and semi-colons.
It will look pretty impressive!

See if you can spot the use of colons and semi-colons in newspapers and magazines.

129

Ellipses

FACTS

An **ellipsis** (…) is often used by a writer when he or she wants the reader to fill in the details. Ellipses can also indicate an unfinished thought, a pause or a nervous or awkward silence in writing. For example: **I knew I'd seen his face before…** Using an ellipsis is a good way of building suspense or mystery in your writing.

Complete each of these sentences by adding words and then ending with an ellipsis.

The three friends ....

The door ....

The castle ....

Behind them ....

Through the forest ....

It was a bone-chilling evening ....

Finish writing this opening paragraph of a story. **Note:** use at least one ellipsis to add an element of suspense or mystery.

Daniel and Leah walked slowly towards the trees. They were excited to have moved house and be living so close to such a huge forest.

....

....

....

....

....

130

Parenthesis: using brackets

Parenthesis is the use of brackets in a sentence to give more information, explain a difficult word, show thoughts or emphasise a point. For example: the girls **(who were very excited)** couldn't wait to get to the zoo.
Parenthesis (plural: **parentheses**) is also another word for **bracket**.

Remove the parentheses from these sentences and rearrange them to create two separate sentences.

Merlin and Doodles (our much-loved pet cats) were fighting when Zoe arrived home.

....

....

The headphones (red and black) were very expensive.

....

....

The boots (made of black leather) were scuffed and dirty.

....

....

For each of these pairs of sentences, rewrite them as one sentence that uses parenthesis.

The graph shows the popularity of each football team. The graph is on the previous page.

....

....

The Eiffel Tower is one of the most iconic landmarks in the world. The Eiffel Tower is found in Paris.

....

....

Bullet points

Bullet points are used to highlight important information within a piece of text, so that a reader can identify the key points and extract information quickly.

Guidelines for using bullet points:

- The text introducing the bullet points should end with a colon;

- If the text that follows the bullet point is not a complete sentence, it doesn't need to start with a capital letter;

- If the text following the bullet point is a complete sentence, it should begin with a capital letter;

- You can end the text following each bullet point with a semi-colon, no punctuation at all, or a full stop if it is a complete sentence. The text following the last bullet point, however, should always end with a full stop.

Here is a picture of Flib-Flob the Alien. Write bullet points to describe him. The first one has been done for you.

This alien:

- has large oval eyes;

- ....

- ....

- ....

Use bullet points to make a list of the main points of a book you have recently read.

The main points are:

- ....

- ....

- ....

- ....

See if you can find examples of bullet points in newspapers and magazines.

Apostrophe to show possession

FACTS

As well as being used in contractions (such as **we'll** and **shouldn't**), apostrophes are used to show possession, or ownership, as in **the peacock's feathers** or **in one month's time**. Apostrophes showing possession can go in two places, depending on the number of possessors. For one possessor, the apostrophe is placed before an added **s**, as in **the cat's food**. This refers to food belonging to one cat. For more than one possessor, the apostrophe is placed at the end of the plural word, as in **the cats' food**. This refers to food belonging to more than one cat.

There are exceptions to these rules. For example: singular words that end in **s** can end with just an apostrophe (') or an apostrophe and **s** ('s).
For example: **Charles' birthday** and **Charles's birthday** are both acceptable.

Draw a line to match each phrase with apostrophes to the number of brothers and friends it refers to. Think carefully before you start.

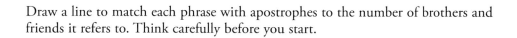

my brother's
friend's clothes

one brother with
more than one friend

my brother's
friends' clothes

more than one brother
and their friends

my brothers'
friend's clothes

one brother and
his friend

my brothers'
friends' clothes

more than one brother
and their friend

Homophones

A **homophone** is a word that is pronounced, or sounds, the same as another word but has a different spelling and meaning. For example: **sun** and **son**.

Read the passage below and underline the homophones that you think have been spelled incorrectly. Then make a list of the correct spellings in the space under the passage.

It was late one wintry Sunday knight. A young elf, with an outrageously long beard and matted hare, was sitting on a toadstool eating magic serial. His friends thought it strange that he liked to eat serial at knight, but even stranger were the contents of the serial! The bowl, witch was full to the brim, contained currents, a peace of would, the herb time and the stumpy tale of a wild bare! The elf didn't really care weather his friends thought it strange. He simply ignored them when they wood pass and stair.

....
....
....
....
....

Words with "ie" and "ei"

FACTS

The spelling rhyme "I before E except after C" is well known, but it does not always apply.

The rule does apply:

- when the letters together make a long **e** sound, as in **deceit** and **shield**.

The rule does not apply:

- when the letters together make a long **a** sound, as in **sleigh**;

- when using the plural form for words ending in **cy**, as in **pregnancies**;

- when the letters **i** and **e** are pronounced as separate vowels in words, as in **science**.

Write the missing **ie** or **ei** in the space provided below. **Remember**: think carefully about the rule and its exceptions before completing the words.

c_ling	polic_s	shr_k
f_ld	pric_r	soc_ty
fr_ght	rec_pt	th_f
frequenc_s	rec_ve	vacanc_s
n_ghbour	r_gn	v_l
p_ce	rel_f	w_ght

Can you think of any exceptions? Here are some clues:

A part of our diet ....

Eerie or strange ....

To grab hold ....

135

Direct speech

Write down what the aliens Bee-Bee and Bo-Bo are saying in the speech bubbles as direct speech. Make sure you put inverted commas around their words, followed by **asked Bo-Bo** or **replied Bee-Bee**.
Remember: start a new line each time a new person, or character, speaks.

Bee-Bee, what time will the space shuttle arrive?

Bo-Bo, I think it will be eight o'clock.

....
....
....

What shall we do tonight?

Have a party!

....
....
....

Are you looking forward to seeing all our friends?

Not really. I like it here with just us two.

....
....
....

Reported speech

You use **reported speech** to write what has been said, but you do not use the exact spoken words. You report it in your own words as the writer.
For example: **Mrs White said that she was so pleased with her class**.

Imagine you are writing a report about the new aliens landing on the planet where Bo-Bo and Bee-Bee live. Using reported speech, write next to the aliens what they said about the new visitors.

I could not believe my eyes!

....
....
....
....

....
....
....
....

Will the new aliens take over our planet?

I think they will be friendly, like us.

....
....
....
....

Now try writing a report of an event you have been involved in, such as a birthday celebration or a sporting event at school.

Formal and informal speech

FACTS

Formal speech is used in official writing and situations, such as legal documents, news reports, business letters and official speeches. **Informal speech** is used in everyday conversations and personal letters or emails.

Read the three different letters numbered 1, 2 and 3. Then, write the corresponding numbers in the three small boxes at the bottom of the page, in order from most formal to least formal (informal).

1   Dear Kayte,

I have been to the beach today and the weather was great. I went swimming! I hope to see you soon,

Lots of love,
Claire

2   To Whom it May Concern,

Today I went to a beautiful beach on the south coast. We were lucky that the weather was really good for this time of year. We also had the opportunity to go swimming, which meant we all got some well-needed exercise. I look forward to hearing from you.

Kind regards,
Ms C White

3   Hi Kayte!

Been to beach. Great weather. Went swimming.

See you soon.
Claire

Most formal   Least formal

Formal and informal speech

Formal and informal writing and speech differ from each other in tone and structure.

Write a letter to your friend telling him or her about your last holiday.
Think about whether you will write the letter in formal or informal speech.

Points of view

FACTS

A story or any other type of writing can be written from different points of view.
If it is written from the writer's point of view, it is said to be in the first person.
For example: **I saw a spaceship in the sky**.
When the point of view is that of an outside observer, it is said to be in the
third person. For example: **Sophie saw a spaceship in the sky.**

Read each sentence below carefully. Write **first person** or **third person** next to each,
depending on the point of view.

Every summer, I look forward to the warm evenings. ....

The hedgehog curled up inside the hollow log.
He got himself ready for the long, sleepy winter. ....

When I heard the birds chirping, I knew it was the break
of dawn. ....

I feel proud of everything my daughter has achieved. ....

Katy knew how well she had done at Irish dancing and
was full of pride. ....

The hairdresser asked Alena, "Just the usual cut today?"
Alena wondered if she should try something new. ....

I am going on holiday soon. ....

Write two sentences: one in the first person and another in the third person.

....

....

a t o J f p c Y s l n A t

Personification

Personification is a figure of speech in which non-human things are described as having human characteristics, as in **the blushing sun** or **the angry storm**. This type of **figurative language** is often used in poetry. It can help create a vivid picture in the mind of the reader.

Read this poem. Extract the lines using personification and rewrite them below.

It's Coming!

I can smell it in the air; I can feel it in my bones,
It's coming!
Light creeps away,
Dark is dawning on us,
Raindrops frown as they start to pummel the colourless pavement,
It's coming!
Whispering trees dance in the howling wind,
It's grey gravel gravitating downwards from the stormy skies above,
It's coming!
Hail starts to break through the thick murky cotton wool,
Cold crystal tears streaming down pale cheek,
It's coming!
Streaks of light strike the innocent houses below.
The tempest is here.

Alisha Charlton (age 11)

....
....
....

Now match each season to its personification below.

Spring	His icy cold fingers cling to the branches.
Summer	His light steps bring new life to everything he touches.
Autumn	Her skin is dry and wrinkled, lifeless and bare.
Winter	Her hair is a blaze of light, shedding warmth to those around her.

Exploring synonyms

FACTS

Synonyms are words with the same or similar meaning, such as **happy** and **content** or **ill** and **poorly**. Words that are synonyms of each other are said to be synonymous.

Draw a line to match each pair of synonyms below.

buy	large
big	on
quickly	purchase
upon	speedily

Write each of the words from the exercise above under one of these headings.

Verb	Adjective	Adverb	Preposition
....	....	....	....
....	....	....	....

Now think of a synonym to go with each of the adjectives below.

dangerous ....

small ....

clever ....

broad ....

wealthy ....

slender ....

a t o J f p c Y s l n A t

142

Synonyms for "said"

FACTS

Synonyms help improve your writing and make it more engaging. For instance, using synonyms of the word **said**, which is often overused, will make your writing more interesting. When doing this, think carefully about how the character is speaking and what is being said.

The characters below are saying something in a certain way. Think of a synonym for **said** that reflects the way they are speaking. Then, write the sentence using the synonym. The first one has been done for you.

What is said	How it is said	Synonym and sentence
"I am going to the Wizardland."	in a happy way	beamed "I am going to the Wizardland!" beamed the girl.
"They said I couldn't climb the magic tree."	in a sad way	....
"It's not my fault!"	in a frightened way	....
"This way, my lady."	as an answer	....

Types of sentence

A **simple sentence** has one subject and one verb. For example: **Phoebe lives in France.**

A **compound sentence** has two main clauses, which could both stand on their own as separate sentences, joined by a connective. For example: **Phoebe lives in France, but I live in England.**

A **complex sentence** has a main clause and one or more subordinate clauses, joined by a connective. A subordinate clause contains a subject and a verb, but it needs to be attached to a main clause because it does not make much sense on its own. For example: **I first met Phoebe in Paris, where I lived as a small child.**

Study the picture below. Then write a simple, a compound and a complex sentence based on this picture.

Simple sentence

....

....

Compound sentence

....

....

Complex sentence

....

....

Clauses and connectives

When a sentence has two clauses, a connective is used to join them together. The clauses may be two main clauses, making a compound sentence, or a main clause and a subordinate clause, making a complex sentence. Common connectives include **and**, **which**, **although**, **after**, **before** and **so**.

Read the sentences below. Draw one line under the main clause, two lines under the subordinate clause and a circle around the connective. Reread the opposite page to help you. The first one has been done for you.

I like apples (and) I like oranges.

I could go the beach or I could stay home.

Zoe wanted some new clothes, so she went shopping.

Peter took three biscuits, which he later gave to Isobel.

Before Zoe went to school, Isobel came round for breakfast.

Amy watched TV after she had finished her homework.

I tried to explain to Anna, although she didn't understand.

Active and passive

Active sentences describe an action done **by the subject.**
    I directed the award-winning film. (an **active** sentence)
Passive sentences describe an action done **to the subject.**
    The award-winning film was directed by me. (a **passive** sentence)

Change these sentences from **passive** to **active**.

The match was won by our team.

Our team ....

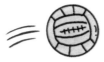   The winning goal was scored by Rachel.

....

The party was enjoyed by all my friends.

....

   Jack was stung by an unusual insect.

....

Now change these sentences from **active** to **passive**.

Aliens invade our planet.

Our planet is ....

Leonardo da Vinci painted the *Mona Lisa*.

....

The team dislike the group leader.

....

The hero piloted his craft with great skill.

....

A hurricane struck the town.

....

Paragraphs and punctuation

Rewrite the following passage in **paragraphs**, **punctuating** it and changing small letters into capital letters where necessary.

Remember: **Paragraphs** separate ideas, themes or instructions. Without paragraphs, writing can be difficult to understand.

rainbows

my heart leaps up when i behold a rainbow in the sky wrote william wordsworth the famous poet and most of us share his feelings when we are lucky enough to see a rainbow there is an old saying that a pot of gold is buried at the end of the rainbow but have you ever tried to reach a rainbows end of course its impossible because a rainbow is really just the result of the raindrops refracting and reflecting light from our sun there are seven colours in the rainbow red orange yellow green blue indigo and violet

....

....

....

....

....

....

....

....

Rewrite this section of a **play script** as a **story**. Use **paragraphs** and **speech marks**. Write on a separate sheet of paper, and continue the story, if you wish.

Remember: When writing **direct speech** (dialogue), start a new paragraph each time the speaker changes.

NICK: It's raining again, but the sun is shining as well.
SOPHIE: I think we should go swimming anyway.
NICK: We might get wet ... let's wait a bit longer.
SOPHIE: We can't swim without getting wet, Nick. What difference does it make?
NICK: Hey!
SOPHIE: What is it?
NICK: Look – a rainbow over the beach!
SOPHIE: Quick, get your spade – we'll be rich!

Maths

Maths test

THE THREE MATHS TESTS ASSESS ARITHMETIC AND
USING AND APPLYING MATHS SKILLS.

Each Maths paper gets progressively harder, with only the
most able children expected to get the final questions correct.
This gives every child the opportunity to do better than a
teacher might expect. It's important to stay positive about
the test, so your child is not disheartened when facing
questions he or she may be completely unable to do.

Taking a test

Paper 1: Arithmetic

This 30-minute test has 36 questions, most of
which score one mark. Children have to work at a
reasonable pace, as they will need to answer at
least one question a minute. Allowing some time
to check through at the end is always a good idea.

▷ The questions are a selection of
calculations, including addition, subtraction,
multiplication, and division, with some
fractions and percentages as well.

Children need to
know to make this
number 1,000
times bigger to
make 2,345,000.

HINTS AND TIPS

Skipping questions

Although skipping a question is
generally not good practice, on this
occasion if children take too long on
one, they may not get time to finish. If a
question is taking too long, encourage
your child to look at the mark, and judge
if it is worth persevering or if it is better
to move on to the next question and
come back to it.

Arithmetic

$40 + 1,000 =$

$345 - 60 =$

$0.04 \div 10 =$

$2,345 \times 1,000 =$

$37.8 - 14.671 =$

$^4/_5 \div 4 =$

$0.9 - 200 =$

$15\% \times 1,000 =$

Paper 2: Reasoning

This 40-minute test is usually on the same day as the arithmetic test, with a break in between. Children are allowed to bring mirrors and protractors, but not calculators. The questions are mostly problem-solving, asking children to use their maths knowledge to work out what sort of calculation to use.

▽ In this question, children will need to identify that there are several parts to solving it. For this example, an addition sum is followed by using subtraction.

At the start of June, there were 1,793 toy cars in the shop.

During June,

8,728 more toy cars were delivered.

9,473 toy cars were sold.

How many toy cars were left in the shop at the end of June?

Paper 3: Reasoning

This second reasoning test is also 40 minutes long, but is taken on a different day. The topics covered are similar to those in the first reasoning test. Children will need to solve problems that require working out a number of steps, without the use of a calculator. After many years of practising these sorts of questions in school, hopefully there will be nothing in the tests that will surprise them.

▷ To solve this problem, first the cost of two mangoes is found by multiplying £1.35 by 2. Then the answer is divided by 3 to find the cost of one pineapple.

Visualizing the problem will help to solve it.

Reasoning

3 pineapples cost the same as 2 mangoes.

One mango costs £1.35.

How much does one pineapple cost?

Preparing for the Maths test

KNOWING CALCULATING METHODS AND SHOWING WORKINGS ARE KEY IN THE MATHS TESTS.

All through school, children will have been taught a whole variety of mathematical methods to deal with different types of questions. They will also be told how, when, and why to apply them, especially in more everyday contexts.

Mathematics is a **creative** and **highly inter-connected discipline** that has been developed over centuries.

The National Curriculum, 2013

Know methods

The teaching of maths today may use very different methods for basic calculations than from decades ago. Many parents feel unable to help their children with maths beyond a certain level. Buying a book that goes through concepts step-by-step, and reading your child's maths homework may help.

▷ Encouraging children to explain to you how they have worked out an answer is one of the best ways of checking they understand it.

Books provide clear explanations to support your child's understanding.

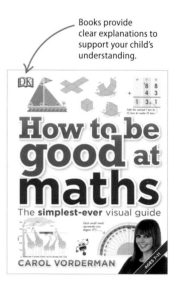

Show workings

In Maths tests, children are often asked to show their workings, and space is given on the paper for this. In some cases, they get an extra mark for showing the correct formal method to solve the problem, even if they get the actual answer wrong.

In this test, **long division** and **long multiplication** questions are worth TWO marks each. You will be awarded TWO marks for a correct answer. You may get ONE mark for showing a **formal method**.

Paper 1 Arithmetic, 2017

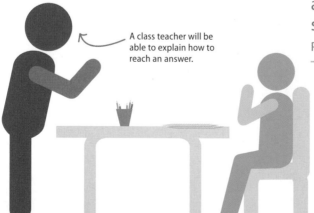

A class teacher will be able to explain how to reach an answer.

◁ Some children find explaining how they have worked out a mathematical problem tricky. This may mean that they don't understand it, and need to ask a class teacher. Other children, who can just think of the answer, may be uncertain how they reached it. They need support to work on explaining in order to gain those extra marks.

Put into practice

Formal maths practice is often given for homework and can also be found in workbooks. Keep the practise time short but frequent. In addition, practical everyday examples of applying maths can be invaluable and fun.

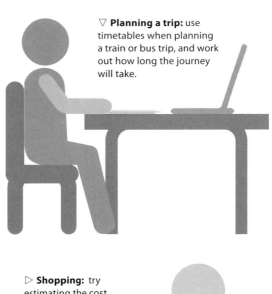

▽ **Planning a trip:** use timetables when planning a train or bus trip, and work out how long the journey will take.

◁ **Cooking:** use measuring and calculating when preparing the ingredients before starting the recipe instructions.

▷ **Shopping:** try estimating the cost of a shop, handling money, and calculating the change.

Special arrangements

Certain students, such as those with a particular disability, are allowed longer time to do the tests. This will have been arranged in advance through the school and the requirement criteria are very specific. For example, children with Type 1 diabetes can have extra time if they have an incidence of low blood sugar during the test. This is because they would be unable to concentrate until their blood sugar levels increased.

Positive and negative numbers

Positive numbers are all the numbers that are greater than zero. Negative numbers are less than zero, and they always have a negative sign (–) in front of them.

Negative numbers have a '–' before them. Positive numbers usually have no sign in front of them.

What are positive and negative numbers?

Move left to count down from zero

–10 –9 –8 –7 –6 –5 –4 –3 –2 –

NEGATIVE NUMBERS

1 If we put numbers on a line called a number line, like the line on this signpost, we see that negative numbers count back from zero, while positive numbers get larger from the zero point.

2 Negative numbers are numbers less than zero. In calculations, we put negative numbers in brackets, like this (–2), to make them easier to read.

Adding and subtracting positive and negative numbers

Here are some simple rules to remember when we add and subtract positive and negative numbers. We can show how they work on a simple version of our numbers signpost, called a number line.

1 **Adding a positive number**
When we add a positive number, we move to the right on the number line.

2 + 3 = 5

To add a positive number, we move to the right

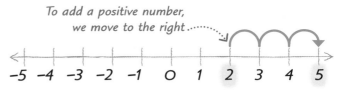

–5 –4 –3 –2 –1 0 1 2 3 4 5

2 **Subtracting a negative number**
To subtract a negative number, we also move right on the number line. So, subtracting –3 from 2 is the same as 2 + 3.

2 – (–3) = 5

To subtract a negative number, we move to the right

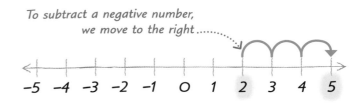

–5 –4 –3 –2 –1 0 1 2 3 4 5

Ups and downs

We sometimes use positive and negative numbers to describe the floors in a buillding. Floors below ground level often have negative numbers.

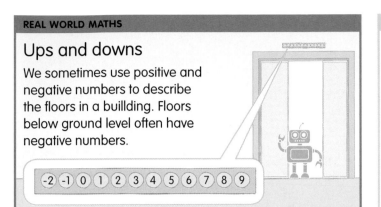

-2 -1 0 1 2 3 4 5 6 7 8 9

Positively puzzling

Use a number line to work out these calculations.

1 $7 - (-3) = ?$ **3** $7 + (-9) = ?$

2 $-4 + (-1) = ?$ **4** $-2 - (-7) = ?$

Move to the right to count up from zero ·········

0   1   2   3   4   5   6   7   8   9   10

POSITIVE NUMBERS

3 Zero (0) is not positive or negative. It's the separation point between the positive and negative numbers.

4 We don't usually put any sign in front of positive numbers. So, when you see a number without a sign, it's always positive.

To subtract a positive number, move to the left on the number line

3 **Subtracting a positive number**
Now let's try subtracting a positive number. To subtract 3 from 2, we move to the left to get the answer.
2 – 3 = –1

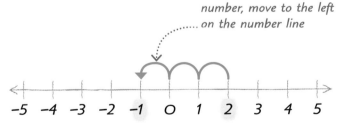

−5 −4 −3 −2 −1 0 1 2 3 4 5

To add a negative number, move to the left on the number line

4 **Adding a negative number**
When we add a negative number, it gives the same answer as subtracting a positive one. To add −3 to 2, we move left on the number line.
2 + (−3) = −1

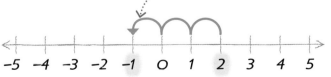

−5 −4 −3 −2 −1 0 1 2 3 4 5

155

Rounding

Rounding means changing a number to another number that is close to it in value, but is easier to work with or remember.

The rounding rule is that for digits less than 5, we round down. For digits of 5 or more, we round up.

Rounding up and rounding down

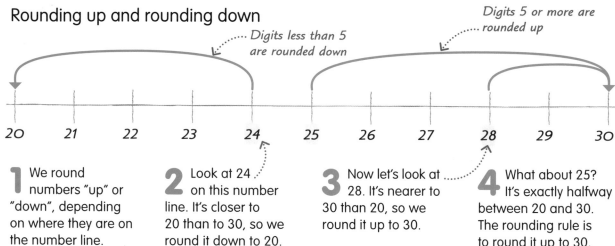

Digits less than 5 are rounded down

Digits 5 or more are rounded up

20 21 22 23 24 25 26 27 28 29 30

1 We round numbers "up" or "down", depending on where they are on the number line.

2 Look at 24 on this number line. It's closer to 20 than to 30, so we round it down to 20.

3 Now let's look at 28. It's nearer to 30 than 20, so we round it up to 30.

4 What about 25? It's exactly halfway between 20 and 30. The rounding rule is to round it up to 30.

Rounding using place value

When we round numbers, we use the place values of a number's digits.

1 Rounding to the nearest ten
We use the ones digit to decide whether to round up or down to the nearest ten. Let's round 83 and 89.

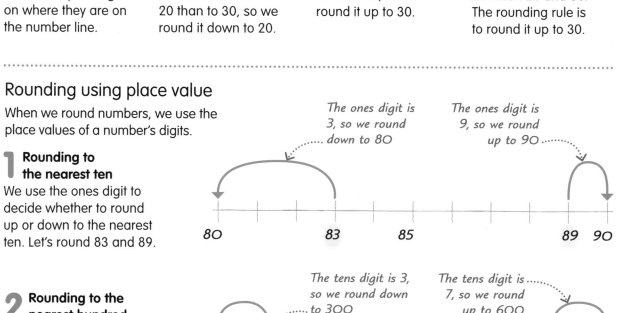

The ones digit is 3, so we round down to 80

The ones digit is 9, so we round up to 90

80   83   85   89 90

2 Rounding to the nearest hundred
To round to the nearest 100, we look at the tens digit and follow the rounding rule. Let's round 337 and 572.

The tens digit is 3, so we round down to 300

The tens digit is 7, so we round up to 600

300 337   400   500   572 600

Rounding to different place values

Rounding to different place values will give us different results. Let's look at what happens to 7641 when we round it to different place values.

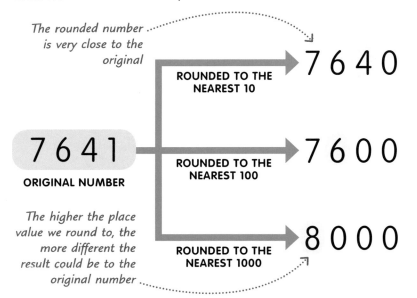

The rounded number is very close to the original

7641
ORIGINAL NUMBER

The higher the place value we round to, the more different the result could be to the original number

ROUNDED TO THE NEAREST 10
→ **7640**

ROUNDED TO THE NEAREST 100
→ **7600**

ROUNDED TO THE NEAREST 1000
→ **8000**

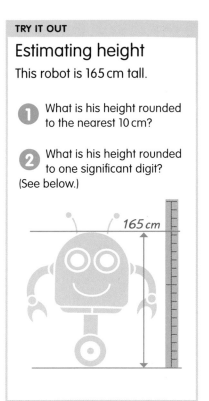
Rounding to significant digits

We can also round numbers to one or more significant digits.

1 Let's look at the number 6346. The most significant digit is the one with the highest place value. So, 6 is the most significant digit. The digit after it is less than 5, so we round down to 6000.

2 The second significant digit is in the hundreds. The next digit is less than 5, so when we round to two significant digits, 6346 becomes 6300.

3 The third significant digit is in the tens column. If we round our number to three significant digits, it becomes 6350.

In a four-digit number, rounding to the most significant digit is the same as rounding to the nearest 1000

6346 → **6000**
ROUNDED TO ONE SIGNIFICANT DIGIT

We round using this digit

This is the second significant digit

6346 → **6300**
ROUNDED TO TWO SIGNIFICANT DIGITS

We use this digit when rounding

This is the third significant digit

6346 → **6350**
ROUNDED TO THREE SIGNIFICANT DIGITS

We round with this digit

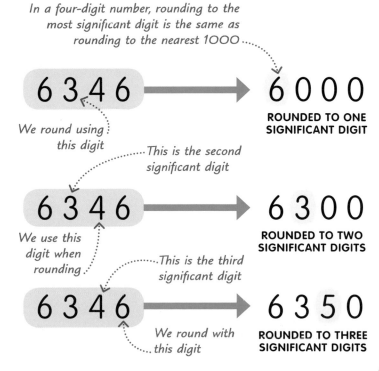

Factors

A factor is a whole number that can be divided or shared into another number. Every number except 1 has at least two factors, because it can be divided by itself and 1.

What is a factor?

This chocolate bar is made up of 12 squares. We can use it to find the factors of 12 by working out how many ways we can share it into equal parts.

$12 \div 1 = 12$

1 If we divide the 12-square bar by one, it stays whole. So, 1 and 12 are both factors of 12.

$12 \div 2 = 6$

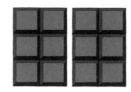

2 Dividing the bar into two gives two groups of six squares. So, 2 and 6 are also factors of 12.

$12 \div 3 = 4$

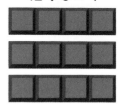

3 When we divide the bar into three, we get three groups of four. So, 3 and 4 are factors of 12.

$12 \div 4 = 3$

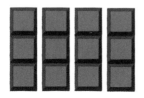

4 When the bar's divided into four, we get four groups of three squares. We already know that 4 and 3 are factors of 12.

$12 \div 6 = 2$

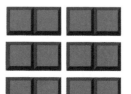

5 Dividing the bar by six gives six groups of two squares. We have already found that 6 and 2 are factors of 12.

$12 \div 12 = 1$

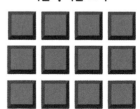

6 Finally, we can divide the bar into 12 and get 12 groups of one square. We've now found all the factors of 12.

Factor pairs

Factors always come in pairs. Two numbers that make a new number when multiplied together are called a factor pair.

$1 \times 12 = 12$ or $12 \times 1 = 12$

$2 \times 6 = 12$ or $6 \times 2 = 12$

$3 \times 4 = 12$ or $4 \times 3 = 12$

1 Let's look again at the factors of 12 we found. Each pair can be written in two different ways.

2 So, the factor pairs of 12, written in either order, are: 1 and 12, 2 and 6, and 3 and 4.

Finding all the factors

If you need to find all the factors of a number, here's a way to write down your findings to make sure you don't miss any out.

1 To find all the factors of 30, first write 1 at the beginning of a line and 30 at the other end, because we know that every number has 1 and itself as factors.

$$1 \times 30 = 30$$

1   30

2 Next, we test whether 2 is a factor and find that $2 \times 15 = 30$. So, 2 and 15 are factors of 30. We put 2 just after 1 and 15 at the other end, just before 30.

$$2 \times 15 = 30$$

1   2   15   30

3 Next, we check 3 and find that $3 \times 10 = 30$. So, we can add 3 and 10 to our row of factors, the 3 after 2 and the 10 before 15.

$$3 \times 10 = 30$$

1   2   3   10   15   30

4 When we check 4, we can't multiply it by another whole number to make 30. So, 4 isn't a factor of 30. It doesn't go on our line.

$$4 \times ? = 30$$

1   2   3   10   15   30

5 We check 5 and find that $5 \times 6 = 30$. So we add 5 after 3, and 6 before 10. We don't need to check 6 because it's already on our list. So, our row of factors of 30 is complete.

$$5 \times 6 = 30$$

1   2   3   5   6   10   15   30

Common factors

When two or more numbers have the same factors, we call them common factors.

1 Here are the factors of 24 and 32. Both have factors of 1, 2, 4, and 8. These are their common factors, in yellow circles.

2 The largest of the common factors is 8. We call it the highest common factor, sometimes shortened to HCF.

The highest common factor is 8

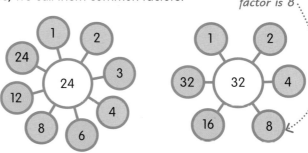

FACTORS OF 24   FACTORS OF 32

159

Multiples

When two whole numbers are multiplied together, we call the result a multiple of the two numbers.

A multiple of a number is that number multiplied by any other whole number.

Finding multiples

The number 12 is a multiple of both 3 and 4

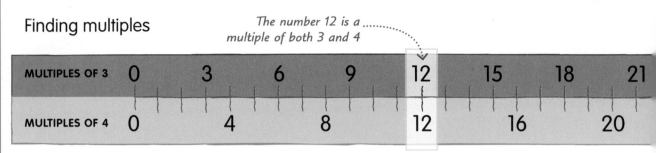

| MULTIPLES OF 3 | 0 | 3 | 6 | 9 | 12 | 15 | 18 | 21 |
| MULTIPLES OF 4 | 0 | 4 | 8 | 12 | 16 | 20 |

1 We can use a number line like this to work out a number's multiples. And if you know your multiplication tables, you'll find working with multiples is even easier!

2 Above the line we have marked the first 16 multiples of 3. To find the multiples, we multiply 3 by 1, then 2, then 3, and so on: $3 \times 1 = 3$, $3 \times 2 = 6$, $3 \times 3 = 9$

Common multiples

We have found out that some numbers can be multiples of more than one number. We call these common multiples.

We call the smallest number in the overlapping section the lowest common multiple

1 This is a Venn diagram. It's another way of showing the information in the number line above. In the blue circle are multiples of 3 from 1 to 50. The green circle shows all the multiples of 4 from 1 to 50.

2 There are four numbers in the section where the circles overlap: 12, 24, 36, and 48. These are the common multiples of 3 and 4.

3 The lowest common multiple of 3 and 4 is 12. We don't know their highest common multiple, because numbers can be infinitely large.

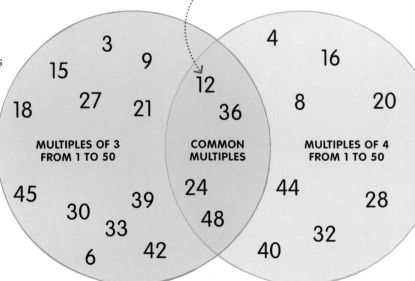

3 9 15 27 21 18

12 36

MULTIPLES OF 3 FROM 1 TO 50

COMMON MULTIPLES

4 16 8 20

MULTIPLES OF 4 FROM 1 TO 50

45 30 33 39 6 42

24 48

44 28 32 40

Multiple mayhem

Which numbers are multiples of 8 and which are multiples of 9? Can you find any common multiples of 8 and 9?

64   **32**   36   **48**
16 81 108   56 90
72 **144**   27 18

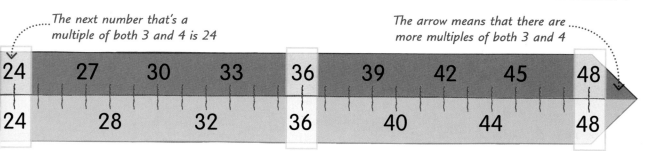

The next number that's a multiple of both 3 and 4 is 24

The arrow means that there are more multiples of both 3 and 4

24   27   30   33   36   39   42   45   48

24   28   32   36   40   44   48

3 Multiples of 4 are marked below the number line. Look at the number 12. It appears on both lines. So it's a multiple of both 3 and 4.

4 Multiples and factors work together – we multiply two factors together to get a multiple. So 3 and 4 are factors of 12, and 12 is a multiple of 3 and 4.

Finding the lowest common multiple

Here's a way of finding the lowest common multiple of three numbers.

1 Let's find the lowest common multiple of 2, 4, and 6. First, we draw a number line showing the first ten multiples of 2.

2 Now we draw a number line showing the multiples of 4. We find that 4, 8, 12, 16, and 20 are common multiples of 2 and 4.

3 When we draw a number line of the multiples of 6, we see that the first common multiple of all three numbers is 12. So 12 is the lowest common multiple of 2, 4, and 6.

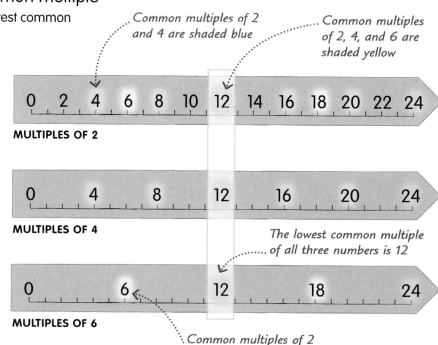

Common multiples of 2 and 4 are shaded blue

Common multiples of 2, 4, and 6 are shaded yellow

0 2 4 6 8 10 12 14 16 18 20 22 24

MULTIPLES OF 2

0   4   8   12   16   20   24

MULTIPLES OF 4

The lowest common multiple of all three numbers is 12

0   6   12   18   24

MULTIPLES OF 6

Common multiples of 2 and 6 are shaded white

Prime numbers

A prime number is a whole number greater than 1 that can't be divided by another whole number except for itself and 1.

A prime number has only two factors – itself and 1.

Finding prime numbers

To find out whether or not a number is prime, we can try to divide it exactly by other whole numbers. Let's try this out on a few numbers.

1 Is 2 a prime number?
We can divide 2 by 1 and also by itself. But we can't divide 2 by any other number. So, we know 2 is a prime number.

$2 \div 1 = 2$
$2 \div 2 = 1$

YES
2 is a prime number

2 Is 4 a prime number?
We can divide 4 by 1 and by itself. Can we divide 4 exactly by any other number?
Let's try dividing by 2: $4 \div 2 = 2$
We can divide 4 by 2, so 4 is not a prime number.

$4 \div 1 = 4$
$4 \div 4 = 1$
$4 \div 2 = 2$

NO
4 is not a prime number

3 Is 7 a prime number?
We can divide 7 by 1 and by itself. Now let's try dividing 7 by other numbers. We can't divide 7 exactly by 2, 3, or 4. We can stop checking once we get over half of the number we're looking at – in this example, once we get to 4. So, 7 is a prime number.

$7 \div 1 = 7$
$7 \div 7 = 1$

YES
7 is a prime number

4 Is 9 a prime number?
We can divide 9 by 1 and by itself. We can't divide 9 exactly by 2, but we can divide it by 3: $9 \div 3 = 3$
This means 9 is not a prime number.

$9 \div 1 = 9$
$9 \div 9 = 1$
$9 \div 3 = 3$

NO
9 is not a prime number

Prime numbers up to 100

This table shows all the prime numbers from 1 to 100.

1	2	3	4	5	6	7	8	9	10
11	12	13	14	15	16	17	18	19	20
21	22	23	24	25	26	27	28	29	30
31	32	33	34	35	36	37	38	39	40
41	42	43	44	45	46	47	48	49	50
51	52	53	54	55	56	57	58	59	60
61	62	63	64	65	66	67	68	69	70
71	72	73	74	75	76	77	78	79	80
81	82	83	84	85	86	87	88	89	90
91	92	93	94	95	96	97	98	99	100

1 is not a prime number because it doesn't have two different factors – 1 and itself are the same number!

2 is the only even prime. All other even numbers can be divided by 2 so are not prime

Prime numbers are shaded dark purple

Non-primes are shaded pale purple

Prime or not prime?

There's a simple trick we can use to check whether a number is prime – just follow the steps on this chart:

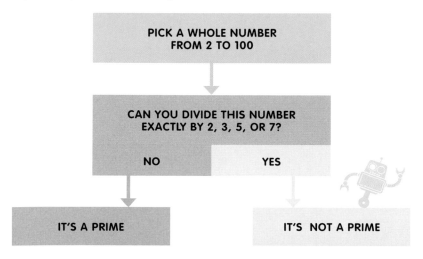

PICK A WHOLE NUMBER FROM 2 TO 100

CAN YOU DIVIDE THIS NUMBER EXACTLY BY 2, 3, 5, OR 7?

NO → IT'S A PRIME

YES → IT'S NOT A PRIME

The largest prime

The ancient Greek mathematician Euclid worked out that we can never know the largest possible prime number. The largest prime we currently know is more than 22 million digits long! It's written like this:

$$2^{74\,207\,281} - 1$$

This means "multiply 2 by itself 74 207 281 times, then subtract 1"

Adding fractions

We add fractions together by adding their numerators (top numbers), but first we have to make sure they have the same denominator (bottom number).

Adding fractions that have the same denominator

To add fractions that already have the same denominator, we just add the numerators. So, if we add $2/5$ to $1/5$, we get $3/5$.

Adding two-fifths to one-fifth makes three-fifths

 +  =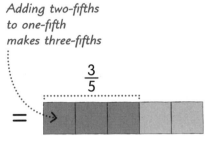

$$\frac{1}{5} \qquad \frac{2}{5} \qquad \frac{3}{5}$$

Adding fractions that have different denominators

1 Let's try the calculation $2\frac{1}{4} + \frac{1}{6}$. First, we have to change the mixed number into an improper fraction.

$$2\frac{1}{4} + \frac{1}{6} = ?$$

2 We change $2\frac{1}{4}$ to an improper fraction by multiplying 2, the whole number, by 4, the fraction's denominator. Then we add 1, its numerator, to make $9/4$. Now we can write our calculation $9/4 + 1/6$.

$$2\frac{1}{4} = \frac{2 \times 4 + 1}{4} = \frac{9}{4}$$

Both numerator and denominator are multiplied by the same number

3 Next, we give our two fractions the same denominators. Their lowest common denominator is 12, so we make the fractions into twelfths.

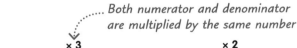

$$\frac{9}{4} \xrightarrow{\times 3} = \frac{27}{12} \qquad \frac{1}{6} \xrightarrow{\times 2} = \frac{2}{12}$$

4 goes into 12 three times, so we multiply by 3   *6 goes into 12 twice, so we multiply by 2*

4 Now we add the numerators of the fractions to make $29/12$. Lastly, we change our answer to a mixed number.

$$\frac{27}{12} + \frac{2}{12} = \frac{29}{12}$$

so

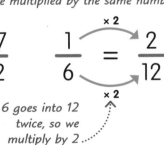

$$2\frac{1}{4} + \frac{1}{6} = 2\frac{5}{12}$$

The improper fraction $29/12$ is changed to a mixed number

Subtracting fractions

To subtract fractions, first we check they have the same denominators.
Then we just subtract one numerator from the other.

Subtracting fractions that have the same denominator

To subtract fractions with the same denominator, we simply subtract the numerators. So, if we subtract ¼ from ¾, we get ²⁄₄, or ½.

Two of the original three-quarters are left

$$\frac{3}{4}$$

$-$

$$\frac{1}{4}$$

$=$

$$\frac{2}{4} \text{ or } \frac{1}{2}$$

Subtracting fractions that have different denominators

1 Let's try the calculation $3\frac{1}{2} - \frac{2}{5}$. As with adding fractions, first we need to change the mixed number and make the fractions' denominators the same.

$$3\frac{1}{2} - \frac{2}{5} = ?$$

2 We change $3\frac{1}{2}$ to an improper fraction by multiplying the whole number by 2, the fraction's denominator, then adding 1, its numerator, to make $\frac{7}{2}$.

$$3\frac{1}{2} = \frac{3 \times 2 + 1}{2} = \frac{7}{2}$$

3 Now we rewrite the fractions so they have the same denominator. The lowest common denominator of $\frac{7}{2}$ and $\frac{2}{5}$ is 10, so we change our two fractions into tenths.

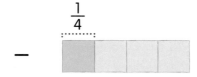

$$\frac{7}{2} \xrightarrow{\times 5} = \frac{35}{10} \quad\quad \frac{2}{5} \xrightarrow{\times 2} = \frac{4}{10}$$

2 goes into 10 five times, so the numerator and denominator are multiplied by 5

5 goes into 10 twice, so we multiply by 2

4 We can now subtract one numerator from the other like this: ³⁵⁄₁₀ − ⁴⁄₁₀ = ³¹⁄₁₀. We finish by changing ³¹⁄₁₀ back into a mixed number.

$$\frac{35}{10} - \frac{4}{10} = \frac{31}{10}$$

so

$$3\frac{1}{2} - \frac{2}{5} = 3\frac{1}{10}$$

Multiplying fractions

Let's look at how to multiply a fraction by a whole number or by another fraction.

Multiplying by whole numbers and by fractions

What happens when we multiply by a fraction? Let's multiply 4 by a whole number, and by a proper fraction. Remember, a proper fraction is less than 1.

The answer is larger than the original number

$$4 \times 2 = 8$$

1 **Multiplying by a whole number**
When we multiply 4 by 2, we get 8. This is what we'd expect – that multiplying a number makes it bigger.

The answer is smaller than the original number

$$4 \times \tfrac{1}{2} = 2$$

2 **Multiplying by a fraction**
Multiplying 4 by ½ makes 2. When we multiply by a proper fraction, the answer is always smaller than the original number.

Multiplying a fraction by a whole number

Let's look at some different calculations to work out what happens when we multiply fractions.

1 Let's try the calculation ½ × 3. This is the same as three groups of one-half, so we can add three halves together on a number line to make 1½.

Three groups of one half make 1½

2 Now let's work out ¾ × 3 on a number line. If we add all the quarters in three groups of three-quarters, we get 2¼.

Three groups of three-quarters make 2¼

3 To work out the same calculations without a number line, we simply multiply the whole number by the fraction's numerator, like this.

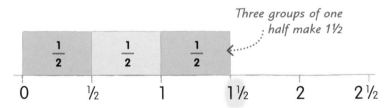

$$\frac{1}{2} \times 3 = \frac{1 \times 3}{2} = \frac{3}{2} \text{ or } 1\frac{1}{2}$$

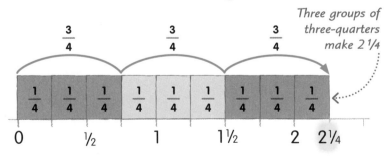

$$\frac{3}{4} \times 3 = \frac{3 \times 3}{4} = \frac{9}{4} \text{ or } 2\frac{1}{4}$$

Multiplying fractions with a fraction wall

When we multiply two fractions together, it can be useful to say that the "×" symbol means "of". Let's find out how this works with the help of a fraction wall.

This section is one-half of the original quarter

1 whole
$\frac{1}{4}$	$\frac{1}{4}$	$\frac{1}{4}$	$\frac{1}{4}$

1 whole

1 whole
$\frac{1}{8}$	$\frac{1}{8}$	$\frac{1}{8}$	$\frac{1}{8}$
$\frac{1}{8}$	$\frac{1}{8}$	$\frac{1}{8}$	$\frac{1}{8}$

1 For the calculation $\frac{1}{2} \times \frac{1}{4}$, let's say this means "one-half of one-quarter". First, let's divide a whole into four quarters and shade in one quarter.

2 Now to find one-half of the quarter, we draw a line through the middle of the four quarters. By dividing each quarter in half, we now have eight equal parts.

3 Let's shade in the top half of our original quarter. This part is one-half of a quarter, and also one-eighth of the whole. So we can say that $\frac{1}{2} \times \frac{1}{4} = \frac{1}{8}$.

$$\frac{1}{2} \times \frac{1}{4} = ?$$

The calculation $\frac{1}{2} \times \frac{1}{4}$ is the same as saying "a half of a quarter".

$$\frac{1}{2} \times \frac{1}{4} = \frac{1}{8}$$

How to multiply fractions

Let's look at another way we can multiply fractions, without drawing a fraction wall.

To multiply fractions we multiply the numerators to make a new numerator. Then we multiply the denominators to make a new denominator.

1 Look at this calculation. Can you see that the numerators and the denominators have been multiplied together to make the answer?

$$\frac{1}{2} \times \frac{1}{6} = ?$$

Multiply the numerators together

$$\frac{1}{2} \times \frac{1}{6} = \frac{1 \times 1}{2 \times 6} = \frac{1}{12}$$

Multiply the denominators together

2 Now let's try with two non-unit fractions. The method is exactly the same – just multiply the numerators and the denominators to find the answer.

$$\frac{2}{5} \times \frac{2}{3} = ?$$

Multiply the numerators together

$$\frac{2}{5} \times \frac{2}{3} = \frac{2 \times 2}{5 \times 3} = \frac{4}{15}$$

Multiply the denominators together

Dividing fractions

Dividing a whole number by a proper fraction makes it larger. We can divide fractions using a fraction wall, but there's also a written way to do it.

Dividing by whole numbers and by fractions

What happens when we divide a whole number by a proper fraction, compared to dividing it by another whole number? Remember, a proper fraction is a fraction that's less than 1.

Dividing by a fraction gives a number that's larger than the original one

$$8 \div 2 = 4$$

1 Dividing by a whole number
When we divide 8 by 2, the answer is 4. This is what we'd expect – that dividing a number makes it smaller.

$$8 \div \frac{1}{2} = 16$$

2 Dividing by a proper fraction
When we divide 8 by ½, we are finding how many halves there are in 8. The answer is 16, which is larger than 8.

Dividing a fraction by a whole number

Why does dividing a fraction by a whole number give a smaller fraction? We can use a fraction wall to find out.

$$\frac{1}{2} \div 2 = ?$$

When a half is divided into two equal parts, each part is a quarter of the whole

1 We can think of ½ ÷ 2 as "one half shared between two". The fraction wall shows that if we share a half into two equal parts, each new part is one-quarter of the whole.

$$\frac{1}{2} \div 2 = \frac{1}{4}$$

$$\frac{1}{4} \div 3 = ?$$

One-quarter can be divided into three, to make three-twelfths

2 Now let's try ¼ ÷ 3. On the fraction wall, we can see that when one-quarter is divided into three equal parts, each new part is one-twelfth of the whole.

$$\frac{1}{4} \div 3 = \frac{1}{12}$$

How to divide a fraction by a whole number

There's a simple way to divide a fraction by a whole number – by turning things upside down!

If we multiply the original denominator by the whole number, we get the new denominator

1 Look at these calculations. Can you see a pattern? We can make the denominators of the answers by multiplying the whole numbers and the denominators together. We can use this pattern to divide by fractions without using a fraction wall.

$$\frac{1}{2} \div 8 = \frac{1}{16}$$

$$\frac{1}{3} \div 2 = \frac{1}{6}$$

$$\frac{1}{4} \div 3 = \frac{1}{12}$$

If we multiply 4 and 3 together, we get 12

2 Let's work out $\frac{1}{2} \div 3$. First, we have to make the whole number into a fraction.

$$\frac{1}{2} \div 3 = ?$$

The whole number becomes the numerator

3 To write the number 3 as a fraction, we make 3 the numerator over a denominator of 1, like this.

$$3 = \frac{3}{1}$$

When we write a whole number as a fraction, the denominator is always 1

The denominator becomes the numerator

4 Next, we turn our new fraction upside down and change the division sign into a multiplication sign. So our calculation is now $\frac{1}{2} \times \frac{1}{3}$.

The ÷ sign changes to a × sign

$$\frac{1}{2} \div \frac{3}{1} = \frac{1}{2} \times \frac{1}{3}$$

The numerator becomes the denominator

5 Now we just have to multiply the two numerators, then the two denominators, to get the answer, $\frac{1}{6}$.

$$\frac{1}{2} \div 3 = \frac{1}{2} \times \frac{1}{3} = \frac{1}{6}$$

TRY IT OUT

Division revision

Now it's your turn! Try out your fraction division skills with these tricky teasers.

1 $\frac{1}{6} \div 2 = ?$ **2** $\frac{1}{2} \div 5 = ?$

3 $\frac{1}{7} \div 3 = ?$ **4** $\frac{2}{3} \div 4 = ?$

Comparing and ordering decimals

When we compare or order decimals, we use what we know about place value, just as we do when we compare whole numbers.

> When we compare decimals, we look at the digits with the highest place values first.

Comparing decimals

When we compare decimals, we compare the digits with the highest place value first to decide which number is larger.

O	$\frac{1}{10}$	$\frac{1}{100}$	
0 .	1		The placeholder, zero, tells us there are no tenths
0 .	0	1	

1 **0.1 is greater than 0.01**
The digits in the ones column are the same, so we compare the digits in the tenths column to find that 0.1 is the greater number.

O	$\frac{1}{10}$	$\frac{1}{100}$	
2 .	6	1	5 is greater than 1 so 2.65 is the larger number
2 .	6	5	

2 **2.65 is greater than 2.61**
This time we have to compare the hundredths columns to find that the greater number of the two is 2.65.

Ordering decimals

Ordering decimals works in the same way as ordering whole numbers.

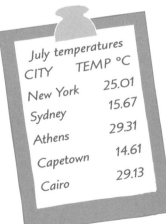

July temperatures

CITY	TEMP °C
New York	25.01
Sydney	15.67
Athens	29.31
Capetown	14.61
Cairo	29.13

We compare the digits in order, starting with the most significant

	T	O	$\frac{1}{10}$	$\frac{1}{100}$
Athens	2	9 .	3	1
Cairo	2	9 .	1	3
New York	2	5 .	0	1
Sydney	1	5 .	6	7
Capetown	1	4 .	6	1

1 Let's help sun-loving Kloog choose a holiday hotspot by putting his list of cities in order, with the highest temperature first. As with whole numbers, we order decimal numbers by comparing their significant digits.

2 To find the greatest number, we compare each number's most significant digit. If they are the same, we look at the second digits, and then, if necessary, the third, and so on. We carry on comparing until we have ordered the numbers.

Rounding decimals

We round decimals in the same way as we round whole numbers (see pages 156-157). The easiest way to see how it works is by looking at a number line.

The rounding rule for decimals and whole numbers is the same: digits less than 5 are rounded down, and digits of 5 or more are rounded up.

1 Rounding to one
This means that we round a decimal to the nearest whole number. So 1.3 is rounded down to 1 and 1.7 is rounded up to 2.

1.3 is nearer to 1 than 2, so we round it down

1.7 is nearer to 2 than 1, so it's rounded up...

1   1.3   1.7   2

2 Rounding to tenths
This means that we round a decimal number to one digit after the decimal point. So 1.12 rounds down to 1.1, and 1.15 rounds up to 1.2.

Digits 4 or less are rounded down

Digits 5 or more are rounded up...

1.1   1.11   1.12   1.13   1.14   1.15   1.16   1.17   1.18   1.19   1.2

3 Rounding to hundredths
Rounding to hundredths gives us a number with two digits after the decimal point. So 1.114 rounds down to 1.11 and 1.116 rounds up to 1.12.

1.114 rounds down to 1.11

1.116 rounds up to 1.12 ......

1.11   1.111   1.112   1.113   1.114   1.115   1.116   1.117   1.118   1.119   1.12

TRY IT OUT

Decimals workout

Here's a list of the racers' times for the slalom skiing race on Megabyte Mountain. Can you round all their times to hundredths, so there are two digits after the decimal point? Who had the fastest time?

FINISH

TWERG	17.239 SEC
BLOOP	16.560 SEC
GLOOK	17.211 SEC
KWONK	16.129 SEC
ZARG	16.011 SEC

Calculating percentages

Per cent means "per hundred". It shows an amount as part of 100. So, 25 per cent means 25 out of 100. We use the symbol "%" to represent percentages. We can find a percentage of any total amount, not just 100. Sometimes we might also want to write one number as a percentage of another number.

Finding a percentage of a shape

We can find percentages of any number. What if a shape has 10 parts or even 20?

1 Take a look at this example. There are 10 tiles altogether. What percentage of the tiles have a pattern?

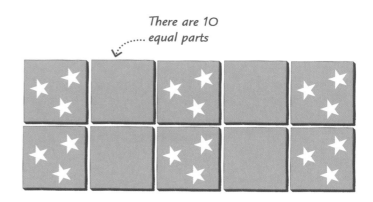

There are 10 equal parts

2 The whole amount of any shape is 100%. To find the percentage represented by one part, we divide 100 by the number of parts (10). This gives us 10, so one tile equals 10%.

$$100 \div 10 = 10$$

Each tile is worth 10%

The total number of tiles

3 We multiply the result (10) by the number of patterned tiles (6). This gives us the answer 60. So, 60% of the tiles have a pattern.

$$10 \times 6 = 60$$

60% have a pattern

TRY IT OUT

Working it out

Here are several shapes. What percentage of each shape has been shaded a dark colour?

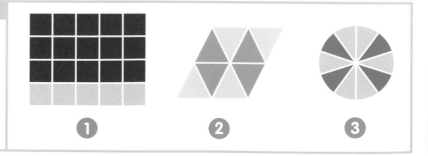

1   **2**   **3**

Finding a percentage of a number

We can also use percentages to divide a number into parts. There's more than one way to do this, but one method is to start by finding 1%.

A percentage is just another way of writing a fraction.

1 Let's find 30% of 300.

$$30\% \text{ of } 300 = ?$$

2 First, we need to find 1% of 300, so we divide the 300 by 100.

$$300 \div 100 = 3$$

...... Divide the total amount by 100

3 Next, we multiply the answer by the percentage we need to find.

$$3 \times 30 = 90$$

4 This gives us the answer: 30% of 300 is 90.

$$30\% \text{ of } 300 = 90$$

The 10% method

In the example above, we began by finding 1% of the total. Sometimes, we can get to the answer more quickly by first finding 10%. This is called the 10% method.

1 In this example, we need to work out 65% of £350.

$$65\% \text{ of } £350 = ?$$

2 We need to find 10% of £350, so we divide the amount by 10. This gives us 35.

$$350 \div 10 = 35$$

3 We know that 10% is 35, so 60% will be 6 groups of 35.

$$6 \times 35 = 210$$

4 We've found 60% of 350. Now we just need another 5% to get 65%. To work out 5%, we simply halve the 10% amount.

$$35 \div 2 = 17.50$$

5 Now add 60% and 5% to find 65%. So, 65% of £350 is £227.50.

$$210 + 17.50 = £227.50$$

TRY IT OUT

10% challenge

Time yourself and see how quickly you can work out the following percentages:

1 10% of 200

2 10% of 550

3 10% of 800

173

Ratio

Ratio is the word we use when we compare two numbers or amounts, to show how much bigger or smaller one is than the other.

Ratio tells us how much we have of one amount compared to another amount.

1 Let's look at these seven ice cream cones. Three are strawberry and four are chocolate, so we say that the ratio of strawberry to chocolate cones is 3 to 4.

Three strawberry cones ..... *Four chocolate cones* ....

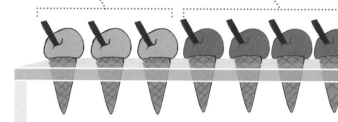

2 The symbol for the ratio between two amounts is two dots on top of each other, so we write the ratio of strawberry to chocolate cones as 3:4.

RATIO OF STRAWBERRY TO CHOCOLATE CONES IS $3:4$

Simplifying ratios

As with fractions, we always simplify ratios when we can. We do this by dividing both numbers in the ratio by the same number.

Simplify the ratio by dividing both numbers by 10

40 g puffed rice cereal

50 g chocolate

$40:50$
÷ 10 ⟶ ÷ 10
$4:5$

$$40 : 50 \quad = \quad 4 : 5$$

1 In this recipe, 40 g of puffed rice cereal, plus 50 g of melted chocolate, makes six mini treats.

2 For every 40 g of cereal we use, we need 50 g of chocolate. So the ratio of cereal to chocolate in the recipe is 40:50.

3 To simplify the ratio, we divide both numbers by 10 to make a ratio of cereal to chocolate of 4:5.

Proportion

Proportion is another way of comparing. Instead of comparing one amount with another, as with ratio, proportion is comparing a part of a whole with the whole amount.

Proportion tells us how much we have of something compared to the whole amount.

Proportion as a fraction

We often write proportion as a fraction. Here are 10 cats. What fraction of them is ginger?

1 Four out of the 10 cats are ginger. So, ginger cats make up four-tenths (⁴/₁₀) of the whole amount.

2 We simplify fractions if we can, so we divide the numerator and denominator of ⁴/₁₀ by 2 to make it ²/₅.

3 So, the proportion of ginger in the whole group, written as a fraction, is ²/₅.

We simplify the fraction by dividing both numbers by 2

$$\frac{4}{10} = \frac{2}{5}$$

÷ 2

÷ 2

Four of the 10 cats are ginger

PROPORTION OF GINGER CATS = $\frac{2}{5}$

Proportion as a percentage

Percentages are another way of writing fractions, so a proportion can be expressed as a percentage, too. What percentage of the cats is grey?

1 There is one grey cat out of 10, so the proportion as a fraction is ¹/₁₀.

2 To change ¹/₁₀ into a percentage, we rewrite it as equivalent hundredths, so ¹/₁₀ becomes ¹⁰/₁₀₀.

3 We know that "ten out of one hundred" is the same as 10%, so the percentage of grey cats in the group is 10%.

One of the 10 cats is grey

We make an equivalent fraction by multiplying both numbers by 10

$$\frac{1}{10} = \frac{10}{100}$$

× 10

× 10

PROPORTION OF GREY CATS = 10%

The order of operations

Some calculations are more complex than just two numbers with one operation. Sometimes we need to carry out calculations where there are several different operations to do. It's very important that we know which order to do them in so that we get the answer right.

BODMAS

We can remember the order that we should do calculations by learning the word "BODMAS" (or "BIDMAS"). It stands for brackets, orders (or indices), division, multiplication, addition, and subtraction. We should always work out calculations in this order, even if they are ordered differently when the calculation is written down.

$$4 \times \mathbf{(2 + 3)} = 20$$

1 Brackets
Look at this calculation. Two of the numbers are inside a pair of brackets. Brackets tell us that we must work out that part first. So, first we must find the sum of 2 + 3, then multiply 4 by that sum to find the total.

$$5 + 2 \times \mathbf{3^2} = 23$$

2 Orders (or indices)
Powers or square roots are known as orders or indices. We work these out after brackets. Here, we first work out 3^2 is 9, then $2 \times 9 = 18$, and finally add 5 to get 23.

$$6 + \mathbf{4 \div 2} = 8$$

3 Division
We work out division and multiplication calculations next. In this example, even though the division is written after the addition, we divide first. So, $4 \div 2 = 2$ and then $6 + 2 = 8$

$$\mathbf{8 \div 2 \times 3} = 12$$

4 Multiplication
Division and multiplication are of equal importance, so we work them out from left to right through a calculation. Look at this example. We divide first, then multiply: $8 \div 2 \times 3 = 4 \times 3 = 12$

$$9 \div 3 \mathbf{+ 12} = 15$$

5 Addition
Finally, we do any addition and subtraction calculations. Look at this calculation. We know that we do division before addition, so: $9 \div 3 + 12 = 3 + 12 = 15$

$$\mathbf{10 - 3} + 4 = 11$$

6 Subtraction
Addition and subtraction are of equal importance, like multiplication and division, so we work them out from left to right. Here, we subtract first, then add: $10 - 3 + 4 = 7 + 4 = 11$

Using BODMAS

If you can remember BODMAS, even calculations that look really tough are straightforward.

1 Let's give this tricky calculation a go.

$$17 - (4 + 6) \div 2 + 36 = ?$$

2 We know that we need to work out the brackets first, so we need to add 4 and 6, which equals 10. We can now write the calculation as: 17 − 10 ÷ 2 + 36

$$17 - 10 \div 2 + 36 = ?$$

3 There are no orders in this calculation, so we divide next: 10 ÷ 2 = 5. So, now we can write the calculation as: 17 − 5 + 36

$$17 - 5 + 36 = ?$$

4 Now we can work from left to right and work out the addition and subtraction calculations one by one. Subtracting 5 from 17 gives 12. Finally, we add 36 to 12 to give 48.

$$12 + 36 = 48$$

5 So, 17 − (4 + 6) ÷ 2 + 36 = 48

$$17 - (4 + 6) \div 2 + 36 = 48$$

TRY IT OUT

Follow the order

Now it's up to you. Use the order of operations and see if you can work out the correct answers to these calculations.

1 $12 + 16 \div 4 + (3 \times 7) = ?$

2 $4^2 - 5 - (12 \div 4) + 9 = ?$

3 $6 \times 9 + 13 - 22 \div 11 = ?$

BODMAS stands for:
Brackets
Orders
Division
Multiplication
Addition
Subtraction

Nets

A net is a 2D shape that can be cut out, folded, and stuck together to make a 3D shape. Some 3D shapes, such as the cube on this page, can be made from many different nets.

A net is what a 3D shape looks like when it's opened out flat.

Net of a cube

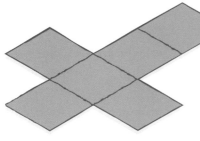

1 This shape, made of six squares, can be folded to make a cube. In geometry, we say the shape is a net of a cube.

Sharp creases help form the shape ......

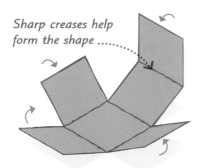

2 The shape is creased along the lines dividing the squares. When the lines are folded, they will form the edges of the cube.

The end square forms the lid ....

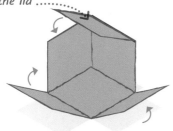

3 The squares round the central square will be the cube's sides. The square furthest from the centre square will be the lid.

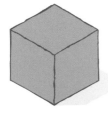

4 The flat net has now been turned into a cube.

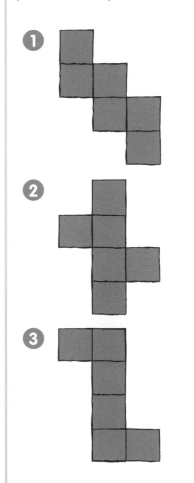

Nets for other 3D shapes

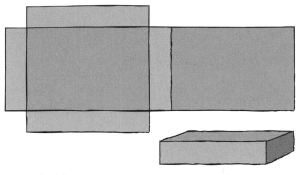

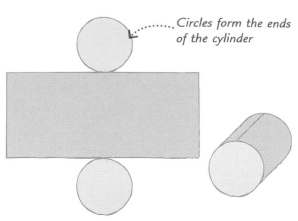

Circles form the ends of the cylinder

1 Cuboid
The net of a cuboid is made of six rectangles of three different sizes.

2 Cylinder
A cylinder's net is formed from just two circles and a rectangle.

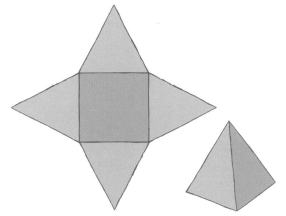

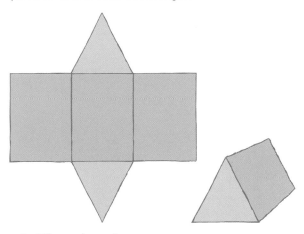

3 Square-based pyramid
One square and four triangles form the net of a square-based pyramid.

4 Triangular prism
A triangular prism is made from a net of three rectangles and two triangles.

REAL WORLD MATHS

Boxes need tabs

When we draw a net for a real 3D shape, we usually include tabs. Tabs are flaps added to some of the shape's sides so that we can stick the box together more easily. If you take an empty cereal box apart, you'll see the tabs that have been glued to some of the panels to form the box.

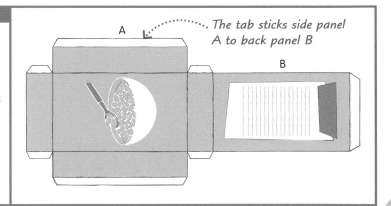

The tab sticks side panel A to back panel B

Using a protractor

We use a protractor to draw and measure angles (differences in direction) accurately. Some protractors measure angles up to 180°, while others can measure angles up to 360°.

> Always place the protractor so its centre is exactly on the angle's vertex (point).

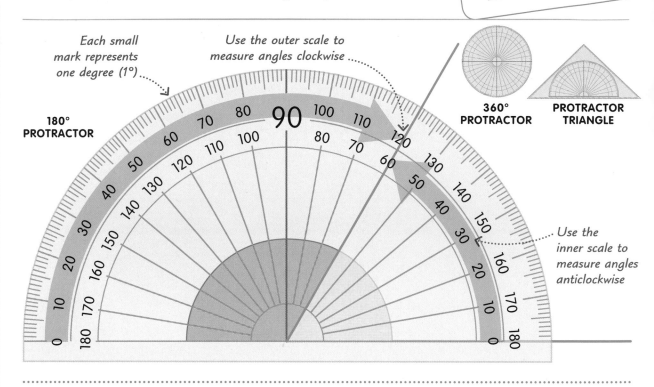

Each small mark represents one degree (1°)

Use the outer scale to measure angles clockwise

180° PROTRACTOR

360° PROTRACTOR

PROTRACTOR TRIANGLE

Use the inner scale to measure angles anticlockwise

Drawing angles

A protractor is essential if you need to draw an angle accurately.

1 Here's how to draw a 75° angle. Draw a straight line with a pencil and ruler, and mark a point on it.

Mark a point on the line

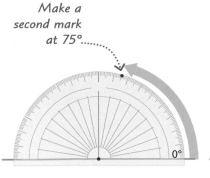

Make a second mark at 75°

2 Put the protractor's centre on the marked point. Read up from 0°, and make a second mark at 75°.

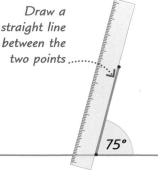

Draw a straight line between the two points

75°

3 Use a ruler and pencil to draw a line between the two points, then label the angle.

Measuring angles up to 180°

You can use a protractor to measure the angle formed by any two lines.

Use the inner scale to measure the smaller angle

Use the outer scale to measure the larger angle

Put the centre of the protractor over the vertex

Make the arms longer if they're not long enough to read

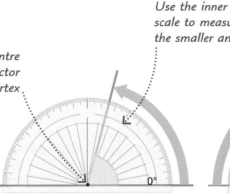
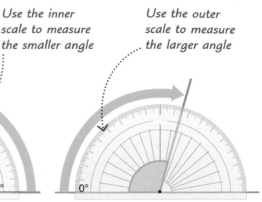

1 Use a ruler and pencil to extend the angle's arms if you need to. This makes it easier to read the angle.

2 Put the protractor along one arm of the angle. Take a reading from where the other arm crosses the protractor.

3 To measure the larger angle, read up from zero on the other side of the protractor.

Measuring reflex angles

Reflex angles are angles larger than 180°. We can use a semicircular protractor to measure a reflex angle if we combine our measurements with what we know about calculating angles.

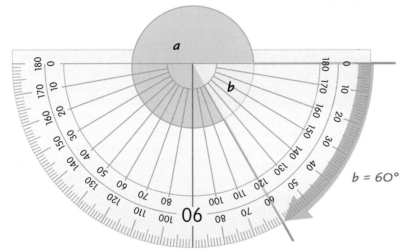

$b = 60°$

1 To find angle a, put the protractor along one arm, facing downwards.

2 When we measure angle b, we find that it's 60°.

3 We know there are 360° in a full turn. So, angle a must be 360° − 60°.

4 So, the answer is a = 300°.

TRY IT OUT

Measure the angles

Practise your protractor skills by measuring these angles. It helps to estimate angles before measuring them – that way, you'll make sure you read from the correct scale.

1

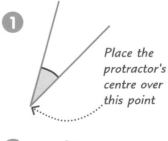

Place the protractor's centre over this point

2

Make sure you read from the correct scale

Angles inside polygons

Polygons get their names from the number of sides and angles they have. We're going to focus on their angles – the difference in direction where their sides meet.

> The sum of the angles inside a polygon depends on how many sides it has.

More sides means bigger angles

All the angles in a regular polygon are the same size. So, if you know one angle, you know them all. Look at these polygons. You can see that the more sides a regular polygon has, the larger its angles become.

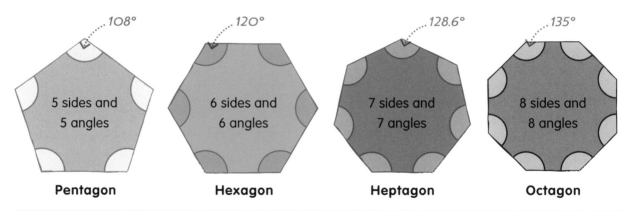

108°

120°

128.6°

135°

| 5 sides and 5 angles | 6 sides and 6 angles | 7 sides and 7 angles | 8 sides and 8 angles |

Pentagon   **Hexagon**   **Heptagon**   **Octagon**

Angles inside regular and irregular polygons

The angles inside polygons with the same number of sides always add up to the same amount. Let's look at the angles inside two different hexagons.

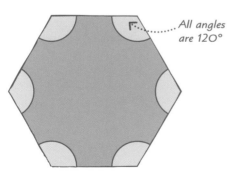

All angles are 120°

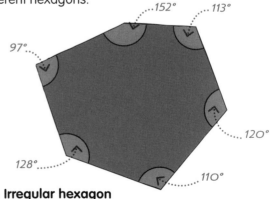

152°   *113°*

97°

120°

128°

110°

1 Regular hexagon
The angles inside this regular hexagon are all the same size. The six angles of 120° add up to a total of 720°.

2 Irregular hexagon
In this irregular hexagon, each angle is different. But when you add them up, the total is 720° – the same as for the regular hexagon.

Calculating the angles in a polygon

To find the sum of all the angles inside a polygon, we can either count the triangles it contains, or use a special formula.

Counting triangles

1 Look at this pentagon. You can see that we can divide the five-sided shape into three triangles.

A pentagon can be split into three triangles

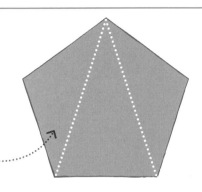

2 The angles in a triangle add up to 180°. The pentagon is made of three triangles, so the angles add up to 3 × 180°, which is 540°

Using a formula

1 Here's a rule about the angles in polygons: the number of triangles a polygon can be divided into is always two fewer than the number of its sides.

2 Let's look at the pentagon again. It has five sides, which means it can be divided into three triangles.

3 So, we can write the sum of the angles in a pentagon like this: (5 − 2) × 180°= 3 × 180° = 540°.

4 There's a formula that works for all polygons. If we call the number of sides n, then:

SUM OF ANGLES IN A POLYGON = (n-2) × 180°

TRY IT OUT

Polygon poser

Combine what you've learned about angles inside a polygon to work out the seventh angle in this irregular heptagon. Remember, if you know how many sides a polygon has, you can work out the sum of its angles.

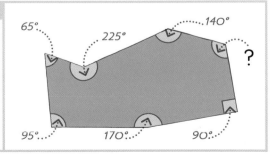

Positive and negative coordinates

The x and y axes on a grid can go either side of zero, just as they do on a number line. On this kind of grid, a point's position is described with positive and negative coordinates.

Quadrants of a graph

When we extend the x and y axes of a grid beyond the origin, we create four different sections. These are called the first, second, third, and fourth quadrants.

Coordinates can be positive or negative, depending on the quadrant they are located in

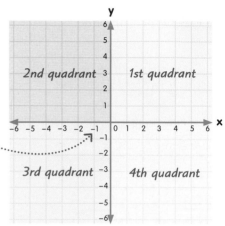

Plotting positive and negative coordinates

Points on a grid can have positive or negative coordinates, or a mixture of both, depending on which quadrant they are in.

1 In the first quadrant, both coordinates are made of positive numbers. Point A is two squares along the x axis and 4 squares up the y axis, so its coordinates are (2, 4).

2 In the second quadrant, point B is 2 squares behind the origin (0,0), so the x coordinate is –2. It's 3 squares up on the y axis, so point B's coordinates are (–2, 3).

3 In the third quadrant, point C is behind the origin on the x axis and below it on the y axis, so both coordinates are negative numbers. The coordinates are (–5, –1).

4 In the fourth quadrant, point D is 6 squares along the x axis and 3 down on the y axis. So, its coordinates are (6, –3).

The x coordinate is negative and the y coordinate is positive

Both coordinates are positive

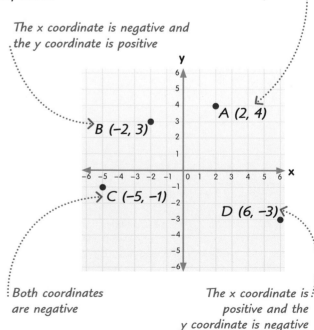

Both coordinates are negative

The x coordinate is positive and the y coordinate is negative

Using coordinates to draw a polygon

We can draw a polygon on a grid by plotting its coordinates, then joining the points with straight lines.

> Remember, positive or negative numbers in coordinates tell us in which quadrant we will find a point.

How to plot and draw a polygon on a grid

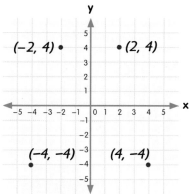

1 We start by plotting these four coordinates on the grid:
(2, 4); (−2, 4); (−4, −4); (4, −4).

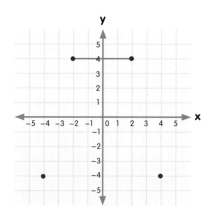

2 Now we use a pencil and ruler to join up the first two points we plotted.

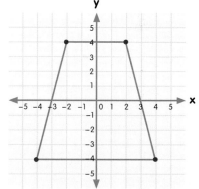

3 We carry on joining up the points until we have made a shape called a trapezium.

TRY IT OUT

Plotting posers

1 Can you work out the coordinates that make the points of this six-sided shape, called a hexagon?

2 If you plotted these coordinates on a grid and joined the points in order with straight lines, what shape would you draw?
(1, 0) (0, −2) (−2, −2) (−3, 0) (−1, 2)

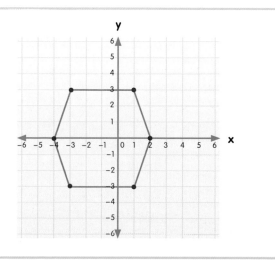

185

Averages

An average is a kind of "middle" value used to represent a set of data. Averages help you to compare different sets of data, and to make sense of individual values within a data set.

The average is the value that's most typical of a set of data.

1 The average age of the Reds football team is 10. Not all the players are 10 years old – some are 9 and some are 11. But 10 is the age that is typical of the team as a whole.

10 10 10 10 10 10

9 9 10 11 11

Average age = 10

·········· Player's age

2 The average age of the Blues football team is 12. Comparing the two averages, we can see that the Blues team is, typically, older than the Reds.

12 12 12 12 12 12

11 12 12 12 13

Average age = 12

3 An average can also tell us if an individual value is typical of the data set or unusual. For example, the Reds' average age of 10 can tell us if these three players aged 9, 10, and 11 are typical of the team or not.

age 9

age 10

age 11

Not typical of team

Typical of team

Not typical of team

Types of average

We can use three different types of average to describe a set of data, such as the heights of a group of giraffes. They are called the mean, the median, and the mode. Each one tells us something different about the group. But they all use a single value to represent the group as a whole. To find out more, see page 187.

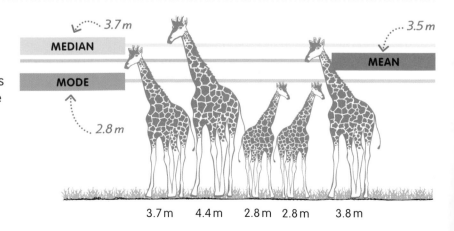

3.7 m

MEDIAN

3.5 m

MEAN

MODE

2.8 m

3.7 m   4.4 m   2.8 m 2.8 m   3.8 m

186

The mean

When people talk about the average, they are usually talking about the mean. We work it out by adding up the individual values in a group and dividing the total by the number of values.

The mean is the sum of all values divided by the number of values.

1 Let's find the mean height of this group of five giraffes.

2 First, we add up all the heights of the giraffes:

3.7 + 4.4 + 2.8 + 2.8 + 3.8 = 17.5

3 Now divide the total height by the number of giraffes: 17.5 ÷ 5 = 3.5

4 So, the mean height of these giraffes is 3.5 m.

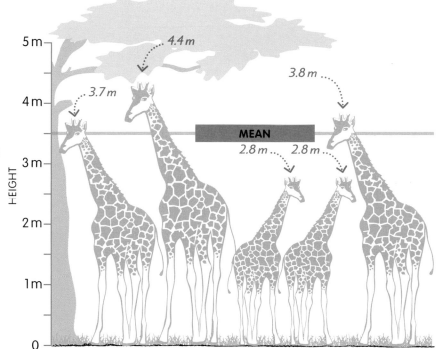

TRY IT OUT

Is it hot today?
Or just average?

Weather forecasts often mention average or mean temperatures. Here are the midday temperatures for a week. Let's work out the mean temperature.

1 First, add up all the individual temperatures.

2 Then count the number of temperatures.

3 To find the mean, divide the total of the temperatures by the number of temperatures.

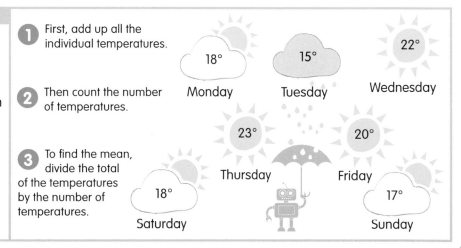

18° Monday
15° Tuesday
22° Wednesday
23° Thursday
20° Friday
18° Saturday
17° Sunday

Line graphs

On a line graph, frequencies or measurements are plotted as points. Each point is joined to its neighbours by straight lines. A line graph is a useful way to present data collected over time.

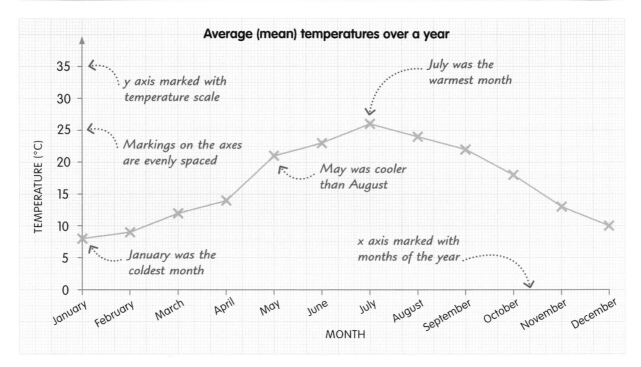

Average (mean) temperatures over a year

y axis marked with temperature scale

Markings on the axes are evenly spaced

July was the warmest month

May was cooler than August

January was the coldest month

x axis marked with months of the year

TEMPERATURE (°C)

MONTH

1 Let's look at this line graph. It shows the average monthly temperatures recorded in Maths Town over one year.

2 The months of the year are listed on the horizontal x axis, and a temperature scale runs up the vertical y axis.

3 The average temperature for each month is plotted with an "x". All the crosses are linked to form a continuous line.

REAL WORLD MATHS

Counting the beats

A heart monitor is a machine that records how fast your heart is beating. It shows the data as a line graph like a wiggly line on a screen or print out.

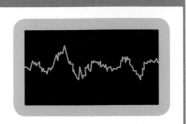

4 The graph makes it easy to see which were the warmest and coldest months of the year. It also lets us compare the temperatures in different months.

Reading line graphs

This graph tells us how Jacob grew between the ages of 2 and 12. We can see how tall he was at any age by going up from the x axis to the line, then across to the y axis. We can also estimate his height between yearly measurements.

1 Let's see how tall Jacob was aged 6. We find 6 on the x axis and then go straight up.

2 When we meet the green line, we go straight across to the y axis. This shows us that Jacob was 110 cm tall at age 6.

3 We can also work out Jacob's height at age 9½. Going up and across, the y axis tells us he was probably 132 cm tall.

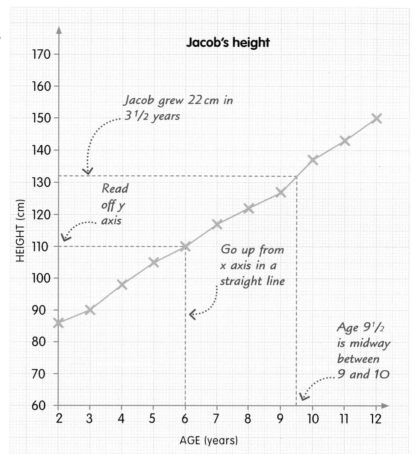

Jacob's height

Jacob grew 22 cm in 3½ years

Read off y axis

Go up from x axis in a straight line

Age 9½ is midway between 9 and 10

HEIGHT (cm)

AGE (years)

Conversion graphs

A conversion graph uses a straight line to show how two units of measurement are related.

1 This graph has kilometres on the x axis and miles on the y axis. The line lets us convert from one unit to the other.

2 To change 80 km into miles, we go along the x axis until we reach 80. Then we go up to the line and across to the y axis, where we read off 50 miles.

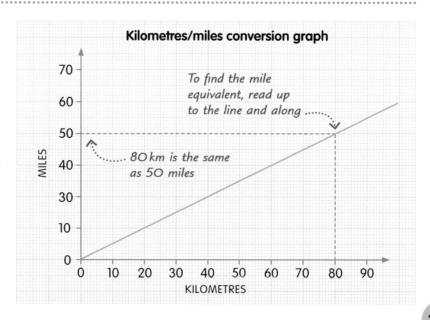

Kilometres/miles conversion graph

To find the mile equivalent, read up to the line and along

80 km is the same as 50 miles

MILES

KILOMETRES

Pie charts

A pie chart presents information visually. It's a diagram that shows data as "slices", or sectors, of a circle. Pie charts are a good way of comparing the relative sizes of groups of data.

> The bigger the slice, the more data it represents.

1 Let's look at this pie chart. It shows the types of film that a group of school children said they most liked to watch.

2 Even though there are no numbers on the chart, we can still understand it. The bigger the sector, the more children chose that type of film.

3 We can compare the film types just by looking at the chart. It's clear that comedies are most popular and science fiction films are liked the least.

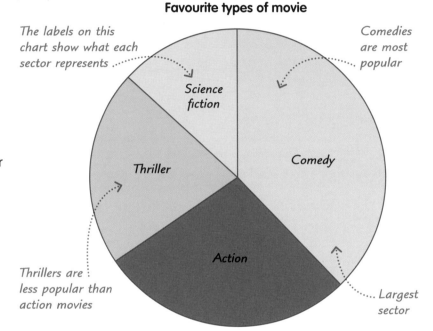

Favourite types of movie

The labels on this chart show what each sector represents

Comedies are most popular

Science fiction

Thriller

Comedy

Action

Thrillers are less popular than action movies

Largest sector

Labelling sectors
There are two other ways of labelling pie charts: using a key or using labels.

KEY

Science fiction

Comedy

Thriller

Action

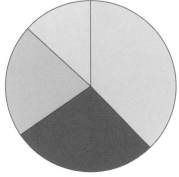

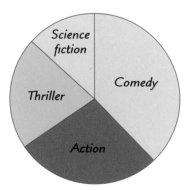

Science fiction

Comedy

Thriller

Action

1 **Key**
We use the colours in the key to find out what type of film each sector represents.

2 **Labels**
We can also write our labels beside the chart or write them on the chart like here.

Pie-chart sectors

The circle, or "pie", is the whole set of data. Each of the sectors, or slices, is a subset. If we add up all the slices, we get the whole pie. We can express the size of a slice as an angle, a proper fraction, or a percentage.

1 Because it is a circle, a pie chart is a round angle of 360°. Each sector that makes up the chart takes up part of this bigger angle.

360°

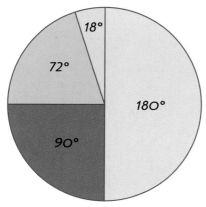

18 + 72 + 90 + 180 = 360°

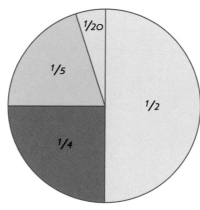

$1/20 + 1/5 + 1/4 + 1/2 = 1$

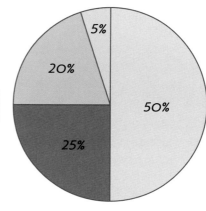

5% + 20% + 25% + 50% = 100%

2 Angles
The angle of a sector is measured from the centre in degrees (°). Together, the angles of the sectors always add up to 360°.

3 Fractions
Each sector is also a fraction of the chart. For example, a sector with an angle of 90° represents a quarter. Together, all the fractions add up to 1.

4 Percentages
Sectors may also be shown as percentages of the whole chart. A sector with an angle of 90° is 25 per cent. Together, the percentages add up to 100%.

TRY IT OUT

Pie-chart puzzles

Here are two problems to solve. Remember that the angles of a pie chart's sectors always add up to 360°, and when expressed as percentages the sectors always come to a total of 100%.

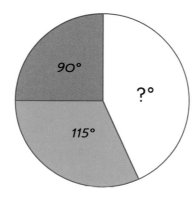

1 Can you work out the mystery angle of the third sector on this pie chart?

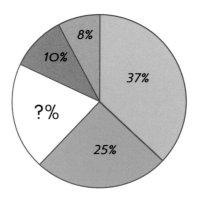

2 What's the percentage of the missing sector on this pie chart?

191

Solving equations

An equation can be rearranged to find the value of an unknown number, or variable.

Simple equations

In algebra, a letter or a symbol represents the variable. We already know that the two sides of an equation must always balance. So, if the variable is on its own on one side of the equals sign, we can find its value by simply carrying out the calculation on the other side.

> It doesn't matter whether a shape or a letter represents the variable.

1 Equations with symbols
Here we have two equations with a shape representing the unknown values. To find the answers we simply multiply or divide.

·········· *The shape represents the unknown value*

$$\triangle = 12 \times 7$$
$$\triangle = 84$$

$$\square = 72 \div 9$$
$$\square = 8$$

2 Equations with letters
In these examples, letters are used to represent the unknown values. The equations are solved in the same way. We just follow the maths sign.

·········· *The letter represents the unknown value*

$$a = 36 + 15$$
$$a = 51$$

$$b = 21 - 13$$
$$b = 8$$

REAL WORLD MATHS

Everyday algebra

We use algebra every day without realizing it. For example, if we want to buy three bottles of juice, two boxes of cereal, and six apples, we can calculate the amount using an algebraic equation as shown here.

$a = £2$

$b = £1$

$c = 50p$

1 We write the equation as:
$3a + 2b + 6c$ = total cost.

2 Now replace the letters with the prices as follows:
$(3 \times £2) + (2 \times £1) + (6 \times 50p) = £11$

Rearranging equations

Finding the value of a variable is harder if the variable is mixed with other terms on one side of an equation. When this happens, we need to rearrange the equation so that the variable is by itself on one side of the equals sign. The key to solving the equation is to make sure it always balances.

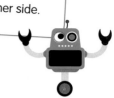

Whatever we do to one side of the equation, we must do the same on the other side.

1 Let's look at this equation. We can solve it in simple stages so that we can isolate the letter b and find its value.

.... Variable

$$b + 25 = 46$$

2 Start by subtracting 25 from both sides and rewrite the equation. We know that 25 minus 25 equals zero. We say that the two 25s cancel each other out.

.... 25 and −25 cancel each other out

$$b + 25 - 25 = 46 - 25$$

3 We are left with the letter b on one side of the equals sign. We can now find its value by working out the calculation on the right of the equals sign.

.... The variable is now the subject of the equation

$$b = 46 - 25$$

4 When we work out 46 − 25, we are left with 21. So, the value of b is 21.

$$b = 21$$

5 We can check our answer by substituting 21 for the letter in the original equation.

.... Both sides of the equation balance

$$21 + 25 = 46$$

TRY IT OUT

Missing values

Can you simplify these equations to find the missing values?

1 $73 + b = 105$

3 $i - 34 = 19$

2 $42 = 6 \times \square$

4 $7 = \triangle \div 3$

193

Formulas and sequences

A sequence is a list of numbers that follows a pattern. By using a formula to write a rule for a sequence, we can work out the value of any term in the sequence without having to write out the whole list.

Number patterns

A number sequence follows a particular pattern, or rule. Each number in a sequence is called a term. The first number in a sequence is called the first term, the second number is called the second term, and so on.

In this sequence, each term is 2 more than the previous term

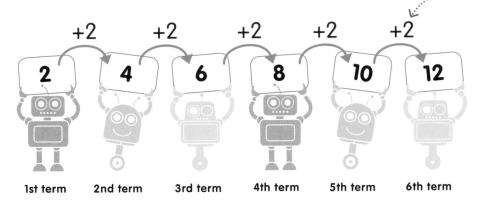

1st term   2nd term   3rd term   4th term   5th term   6th term

The nth term

In algebra, the value of an unknown term in a sequence is known as the nth term – the "n" stands for the unknown value. We can write a formula called a general term of the sequence to work out the value of any term.

The unknown term is called the nth term

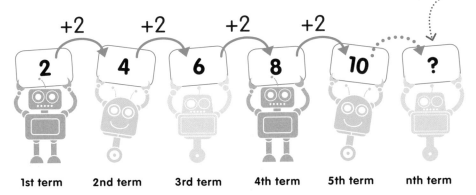

1st term   2nd term   3rd term   4th term   5th term   nth term

The dots show that the sequenc[e] goes on forever

Simple sequences

To find the formula for any sequence, we need to look at the pattern. Some sequences have an obvious pattern, so we can easily find the rule and write it as a formula.

The rule is multiply the term by 4

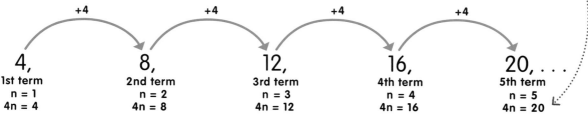

4,	8,	12,	16,	20, . . .
1st term	**2nd term**	**3rd term**	**4th term**	**5th term**
n = 1	n = 2	n = 3	n = 4	n = 5
4n = 4	4n = 8	4n = 12	4n = 16	4n = 20

1 This sequence is made up of the multiples of 4. So, we can say the nth term is 4 × n. In algebra, we write this as 4n.

2 So, to find the value of the 30th term for example, we simply replace n in the formula with 30 and perform the calculation 4 × 30 = 120.

Two-step formulas

Some sequences will follow two steps such as multiplying and subtracting, or multiplying and adding.

The rule is multiply the term by 5, then subtract 1

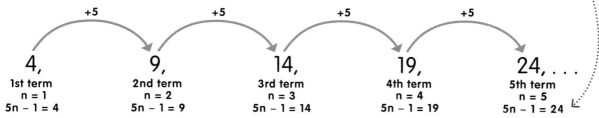

4,	9,	14,	19,	24, . . .
1st term	**2nd term**	**3rd term**	**4th term**	**5th term**
n = 1	n = 2	n = 3	n = 4	n = 5
5n − 1 = 4	5n − 1 = 9	5n − 1 = 14	5n − 1 = 19	5n − 1 = 24

1 The formula for this sequence is 5n − 1. So, to find any term in the sequence, we have to perform a multiplication followed by a subtraction.

2 To find the 50th term in the sequence, for example, we replace n in the formula with 50. Then we can write 5 × 50 − 1 = 249. So, the 50th term is 249.

TRY IT OUT

Finding terms

The formula to work out the nth term in this sequence is 6n + 2. Can you continue the sequence and apply the formula?

8,   14,   20,   26,   32,   38,...

1 Write the next five numbers in this sequence.

2 Calculate the value of the 40th term.

3 Calculate the value of the 100th term.

Two-dimensional shapes

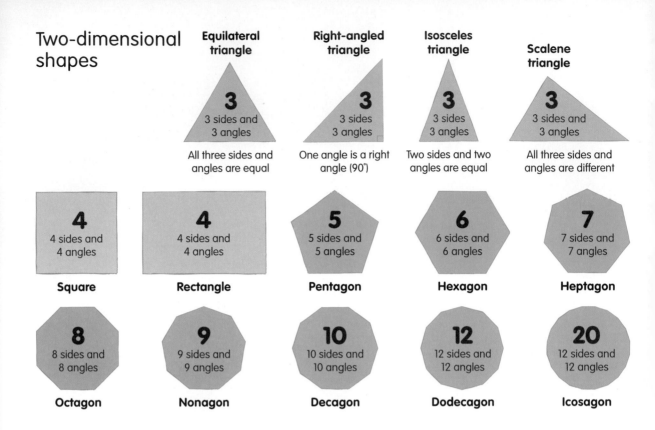

Equilateral triangle

3
3 sides and
3 angles

All three sides and
angles are equal

Right-angled triangle

3
3 sides
3 angles

One angle is a right
angle (90°)

Isosceles triangle

3
3 sides
3 angles

Two sides and two
angles are equal

Scalene triangle

3
3 sides and
3 angles

All three sides and
angles are different

4
4 sides and
4 angles

Square

4
4 sides and
4 angles

Rectangle

5
5 sides and
5 angles

Pentagon

6
6 sides and
6 angles

Hexagon

7
7 sides and
7 angles

Heptagon

8
8 sides and
8 angles

Octagon

9
9 sides and
9 angles

Nonagon

10
10 sides and
10 angles

Decagon

12
12 sides and
12 angles

Dodecagon

20
12 sides and
12 angles

Icosagon

Parts of a circle

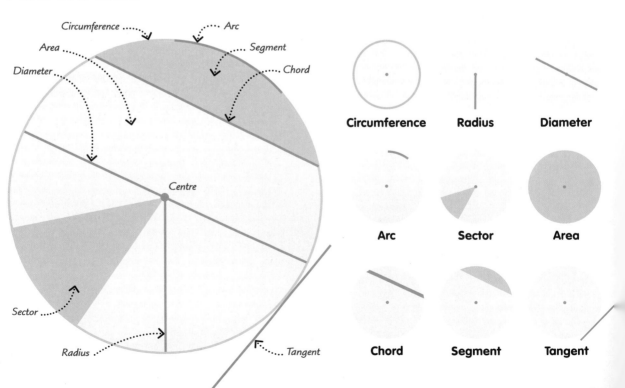

Circumference

Arc

Area

Segment

Diameter

Chord

Centre

Sector

Radius

Tangent

Circumference

Radius

Diameter

Arc

Sector

Area

Chord

Tangent

Three-dimensional shapes

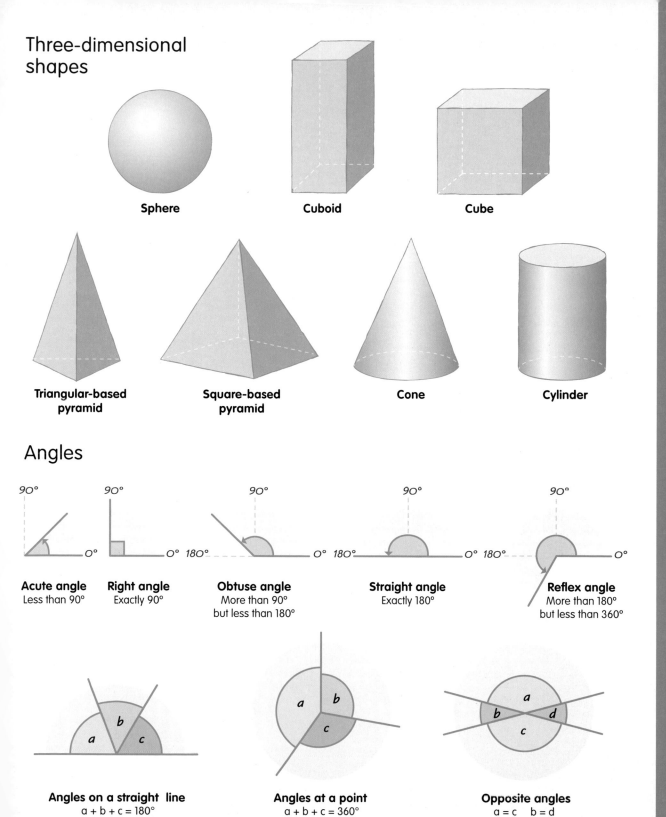

Sphere

Cuboid

Cube

Triangular-based pyramid

Square-based pyramid

Cone

Cylinder

Angles

Acute angle
Less than 90°

Right angle
Exactly 90°

Obtuse angle
More than 90°
but less than 180°

Straight angle
Exactly 180°

Reflex angle
More than 180°
but less than 360°

Angles on a straight line
a + b + c = 180°

Angles at a point
a + b + c = 360°

Opposite angles
a = c   b = d

Multiplication tables

1× table	2× table	3× table	4× table	5× table	6× table
1 × 0 = **0**	2 × 0 = **0**	3 × 0 = **0**	4 × 0 = **0**	5 × 0 = **0**	6 × 0 = **0**
1 × 1 = **1**	2 × 1 = **2**	3 × 1 = **3**	4 × 1 = **4**	5 × 1 = **5**	6 × 1 = **6**
1 × 2 = **2**	2 × 2 = **4**	3 × 2 = **6**	4 × 2 = **8**	5 × 2 = **10**	6 × 2 = **12**
1 × 3 = **3**	2 × 3 = **6**	3 × 3 = **9**	4 × 3 = **12**	5 × 3 = **15**	6 × 3 = **18**
1 × 4 = **4**	2 × 4 = **8**	3 × 4 = **12**	4 × 4 = **16**	5 × 4 = **20**	6 × 4 = **24**
1 × 5 = **5**	2 × 5 = **10**	3 × 5 = **15**	4 × 5 = **20**	5 × 5 = **25**	6 × 5 = **30**
1 × 6 = **6**	2 × 6 = **12**	3 × 6 = **18**	4 × 6 = **24**	5 × 6 = **30**	6 × 6 = **36**
1 × 7 = **7**	2 × 7 = **14**	3 × 7 = **21**	4 × 7 = **28**	5 × 7 = **35**	6 × 7 = **42**
1 × 8 = **8**	2 × 8 = **16**	3 × 8 = **24**	4 × 8 = **32**	5 × 8 = **40**	6 × 8 = **48**
1 × 9 = **9**	2 × 9 = **18**	3 × 9 = **27**	4 × 9 = **36**	5 × 9 = **45**	6 × 9 = **54**
1 × 10 = **10**	2 × 10 = **20**	3 × 10 = **30**	4 × 10 = **40**	5 × 10 = **50**	6 × 10 = **60**
1 × 11 = **11**	2 × 11 = **22**	3 × 11 = **33**	4 × 11 = **44**	5 × 11 = **55**	6 × 11 = **66**
1 × 12 = **12**	2 × 12 = **24**	3 × 12 = **36**	4 × 12 = **48**	5 × 12 = **60**	6 × 12 = **72**

The fraction wall

1 whole												
$\frac{1}{2}$ || $\frac{1}{2}$ ||
$\frac{1}{3}$	$\frac{1}{3}$	$\frac{1}{3}$	
$\frac{1}{4}$	$\frac{1}{4}$	$\frac{1}{4}$	$\frac{1}{4}$
$\frac{1}{5}$	$\frac{1}{5}$	$\frac{1}{5}$	$\frac{1}{5}$	$\frac{1}{5}$
$\frac{1}{6}$	$\frac{1}{6}$	$\frac{1}{6}$	$\frac{1}{6}$	$\frac{1}{6}$	$\frac{1}{6}$
$\frac{1}{8}$	$\frac{1}{8}$	$\frac{1}{8}$	$\frac{1}{8}$	$\frac{1}{8}$	$\frac{1}{8}$	$\frac{1}{8}$	$\frac{1}{8}$
$\frac{1}{10}$	$\frac{1}{10}$	$\frac{1}{10}$	$\frac{1}{10}$	$\frac{1}{10}$	$\frac{1}{10}$	$\frac{1}{10}$	$\frac{1}{10}$	$\frac{1}{10}$	$\frac{1}{10}$
$\frac{1}{12}$	$\frac{1}{12}$	$\frac{1}{12}$	$\frac{1}{12}$	$\frac{1}{12}$	$\frac{1}{12}$	$\frac{1}{12}$	$\frac{1}{12}$	$\frac{1}{12}$	$\frac{1}{12}$	$\frac{1}{12}$	$\frac{1}{12}$

Fractions, decimals, and percentages

Percentage	Decimal	Fraction
1%	0.01	$\frac{1}{100}$
5%	0.05	$\frac{5}{100}$
10%	0.1	$\frac{1}{10}$
20%	0.2	$\frac{1}{5}$
25%	0.25	$\frac{1}{4}$
50%	0.5	$\frac{1}{2}$
75%	0.75	$\frac{3}{4}$
100%	1	$\frac{100}{100}$

The multiplication grid

×	1	2	3	4	5	6	7	8	9	10	11	12
1	1	2	3	4	5	6	7	8	9	10	11	12
2	2	4	6	8	10	12	14	16	18	20	22	24
3	3	6	9	12	15	18	21	24	27	30	33	36
4	4	8	12	16	20	24	28	32	36	40	44	48
5	5	10	15	20	25	30	35	40	45	50	55	60
6	6	12	18	24	30	36	42	48	54	60	66	72
7	7	14	21	28	35	42	49	56	63	70	77	84
8	8	16	24	32	40	48	56	64	72	80	88	96
9	9	18	27	36	45	54	63	72	81	90	99	108
10	10	20	30	40	50	60	70	80	90	100	110	120
11	11	22	33	44	55	66	77	88	99	110	121	132
12	12	24	36	48	60	72	84	96	108	120	132	144

Prime numbers up to 100

1	2	3	4	5	6	7	8	9	10
11	12	13	14	15	16	17	18	19	20
21	22	23	24	25	26	27	28	29	30
31	32	33	34	35	36	37	38	39	40
41	42	43	44	45	46	47	48	49	50
51	52	53	54	55	56	57	58	59	60
61	62	63	64	65	66	67	68	69	70
71	72	73	74	75	76	77	78	79	80
81	82	83	84	85	86	87	88	89	90
91	92	93	94	95	96	97	98	99	100

7× table	8× table	9× table	10× table	11× table	12× table
7 × 0 = **0**	8 × 0 = **0**	9 × 0 = **0**	10 × 0 = **0**	11 × 0 = **0**	12 × 0 = **0**
7 × 1 = **7**	8 × 1 = **8**	9 × 1 = **9**	10 × 1 = **10**	11 × 1 = **11**	12 × 1 = **12**
7 × 2 = **14**	8 × 2 = **16**	9 × 2 = **18**	10 × 2 = **20**	11 × 2 = **22**	12 × 2 = **24**
7 × 3 = **21**	8 × 3 = **24**	9 × 3 = **27**	10 × 3 = **30**	11 × 3 = **33**	12 × 3 = **36**
7 × 4 = **28**	8 × 4 = **32**	9 × 4 = **36**	10 × 4 = **40**	11 × 4 = **44**	12 × 4 = **48**
7 × 5 = **35**	8 × 5 = **40**	9 × 5 = **45**	10 × 5 = **50**	11 × 5 = **55**	12 × 5 = **60**
7 × 6 = **42**	8 × 6 = **48**	9 × 6 = **54**	10 × 6 = **60**	11 × 6 = **66**	12 × 6 = **72**
7 × 7 = **49**	8 × 7 = **56**	9 × 7 = **63**	10 × 7 = **70**	11 × 7 = **77**	12 × 7 = **84**
7 × 8 = **56**	8 × 8 = **64**	9 × 8 = **72**	10 × 8 = **80**	11 × 8 = **88**	12 × 8 = **96**
7 × 9 = **63**	8 × 9 = **72**	9 × 9 = **81**	10 × 9 = **90**	11 × 9 = **99**	12 × 9 = **108**
7 × 10 = **70**	8 × 10 = **80**	9 × 10 = **90**	10 × 10 = **100**	11 × 10 = **110**	12 × 10 = **120**
7 × 11 = **77**	8 × 11 = **88**	9 × 11 = **99**	10 × 11 = **110**	11 × 11 = **121**	12 × 11 = **132**
7 × 12 = **84**	8 × 12 = **96**	9 × 12 = **108**	10 × 12 = **120**	11 × 12 = **132**	12 × 12 = **144**

Metric units of length

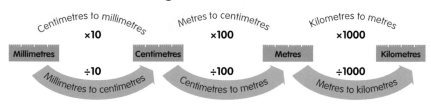

Metric units of capacity

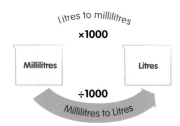

Metric units of mass

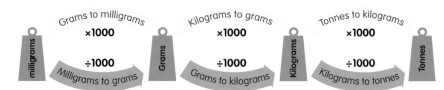

Formulas for perimeter (the distance around the edge of a shape)

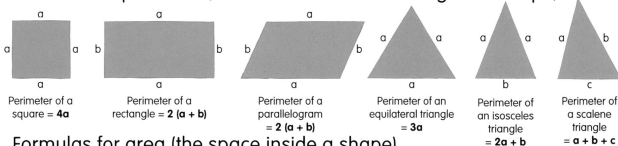

Perimeter of a square = **4a**

Perimeter of a rectangle = **2 (a + b)**

Perimeter of a parallelogram = **2 (a + b)**

Perimeter of an equilateral triangle = **3a**

Perimeter of an isosceles triangle = **2a + b**

Perimeter of a scalene triangle = **a + b + c**

Formulas for area (the space inside a shape)

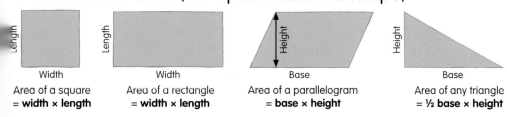

Area of a square = **width × length**

Area of a rectangle = **width × length**

Area of a parallelogram = **base × height**

Area of any triangle = **½ base × height**

Factors, multiples, and prime numbers

Write all the factors of these numbers.

12	1, 2, 3, 4, 6, 12	18	1, 2, 3, 6, 9, 18
25	1, 5, 25	64	1, 2, 4, 8, 16, 32, 64
72	1, 2, 3, 4, 6, 8, 9, 12, 18, 24, 36, 72	96	1, 2, 3, 4, 6, 8, 12, 16, 24, 32, 48, 96

What are the common factors of these numbers?

15 and 25

72 and 108

48 and 64

150 and 125

Circle the multiples of these numbers.

Multiples of 3

Multiples of 5

Multiples of 8

Write the first three common multiples of these numbers.

3 and 5

4 and 7

Write the prime numbers between these numbers.

1 and 20

20 and 50

Add and subtract fractions

Work out these calculations.

$$\frac{1}{4} + \frac{5}{6} = \frac{3}{12} + \frac{10}{12} = \frac{13}{12} = 1\frac{1}{12}$$

$$\frac{7}{9} - \frac{2}{3} = \frac{7}{9} - \frac{6}{9} = \frac{1}{9}$$

Remember: Use equivalent fractions to make the denominators the same.

Add these fractions. Give answers as improper fractions if necessary.

$$\frac{1}{3} + \frac{1}{3} = \qquad \frac{4}{11} + \frac{3}{4} = \qquad \frac{6}{9} + \frac{12}{18} = \qquad \frac{3}{5} + \frac{4}{10} =$$

$$\frac{3}{8} + \frac{2}{8} = \qquad \frac{1}{5} + \frac{3}{5} = \qquad \frac{2}{5} + \frac{6}{15} = \qquad \frac{4}{7} + \frac{2}{5} =$$

$$\frac{2}{6} + \frac{3}{12} = \qquad \frac{5}{9} + \frac{3}{9} = \qquad \frac{2}{7} + \frac{4}{7} = \qquad \frac{2}{5} + \frac{3}{9} =$$

$$\frac{5}{8} + \frac{4}{12} = \qquad \frac{1}{4} + \frac{3}{8} = \qquad \frac{4}{10} + \frac{3}{10} =$$

Add these mixed fractions. Give answers as mixed fractions.
Remember: First change them to improper fractions.

$$1\frac{1}{4} + 3\frac{1}{4} = \qquad 3\frac{1}{3} + 4\frac{1}{2} = \qquad 2\frac{2}{5} + 2\frac{3}{5} =$$

$$2\frac{3}{4} + 1\frac{2}{3} = \qquad 1\frac{4}{5} + 3\frac{3}{10} = \qquad 4\frac{5}{8} + 2\frac{3}{4} =$$

Subtract these fractions. Write answers in simplest form.

$$\frac{3}{5} - \frac{2}{5} = \qquad \frac{3}{4} - \frac{7}{12} = \qquad \frac{3}{5} - \frac{1}{3} = \qquad \frac{1}{3} - \frac{1}{4} =$$

$$\frac{4}{5} - \frac{7}{10} = \qquad \frac{5}{8} - \frac{3}{8} = \qquad \frac{11}{15} - \frac{2}{5} = \qquad \frac{1}{2} - \frac{2}{7} =$$

$$\frac{2}{3} - \frac{4}{9} = \qquad \frac{5}{6} - \frac{2}{3} = \qquad \frac{7}{9} - \frac{2}{9} = \qquad \frac{1}{2} - \frac{5}{12} =$$

Subtract these mixed fractions. Give answers in simplest form.
Remember: First change them to improper fractions.

$$4\frac{2}{5} - 3\frac{4}{5} = \qquad 2\frac{5}{8} - 1\frac{7}{8} = \qquad 5\frac{4}{9} - 4\frac{2}{9} =$$

$$2\frac{2}{3} - 1\frac{3}{4} = \qquad 2\frac{1}{2} - 2\frac{3}{8} = \qquad 4\frac{5}{6} - 3\frac{2}{3} =$$

Multiply fractions

Work out these calculations.

$$\frac{2}{3} \times \frac{1}{2} = \frac{2 \times 1}{3 \times 2} = \frac{2}{6} = \frac{1}{3}$$

$$\frac{2}{5} \times 2 = \frac{2}{5} \times \frac{2}{1} = \frac{2 \times 2}{5 \times 1} = \frac{4}{5}$$

Multiply these fractions. Give answers in their simplest form.

$\frac{3}{4} \times \frac{1}{2} =$ 　　　　　$\frac{3}{5} \times \frac{2}{3} =$

$\frac{3}{10} \times \frac{2}{5} =$ 　　　　　$\frac{1}{2} \times \frac{3}{7} =$

$\frac{2}{3} \times \frac{1}{4} =$ 　　　　　$\frac{5}{8} \times \frac{2}{4} =$

$\frac{7}{10} \times \frac{3}{4} =$ 　　　　　$\frac{1}{2} \times \frac{5}{8} =$

$\frac{2}{3} \times \frac{4}{10} =$ 　　　　　$\frac{3}{5} \times \frac{2}{6} =$

$\frac{4}{9} \times \frac{1}{3} =$ 　　　　　$\frac{2}{3} \times \frac{5}{6} =$

Multiply these fractions by whole numbers. Give answers as mixed fractions.

$\frac{2}{3} \times 4 =$ 　　　　　$\frac{3}{5} \times 2 =$

$\frac{3}{4} \times 6 =$ 　　　　　$\frac{3}{10} \times 5 =$

$\frac{5}{8} \times 3 =$ 　　　　　$\frac{4}{7} \times 8 =$

$\frac{1}{5} \times 9 =$ 　　　　　$\frac{1}{4} \times 4 =$

$\frac{5}{12} \times 3 =$ 　　　　　$\frac{6}{11} \times 2 =$

$\frac{5}{9} \times 3 =$ 　　　　　$\frac{10}{100} \times 4 =$

Divide fractions

Divide these fractions by whole numbers. Give answers in their simplest form.

$$\frac{1}{3} \div 3 = \qquad\qquad \frac{4}{5} \div 2 =$$

$$\frac{3}{8} \div 2 = \qquad\qquad \frac{1}{4} \div 6 =$$

$$\frac{1}{2} \div 5 = \qquad\qquad \frac{3}{4} \div 7 =$$

$$\frac{7}{10} \div 3 = \qquad\qquad \frac{2}{9} \div 5 =$$

$$\frac{3}{7} \div 3 = \qquad\qquad \frac{2}{5} \div 4 =$$

$$\frac{2}{3} \div 6 = \qquad\qquad \frac{5}{6} \div 3 =$$

Divide these fractions. Give answers as a mixed number if needed.

$$\frac{1}{2} \div \frac{1}{3} = \qquad\qquad \frac{3}{4} \div \frac{2}{3} =$$

$$\frac{3}{5} \div \frac{1}{6} = \qquad\qquad \frac{5}{7} \div \frac{2}{5} =$$

$$\frac{2}{9} \div \frac{3}{5} = \qquad\qquad \frac{5}{8} \div \frac{1}{2} =$$

$$\frac{7}{10} \div \frac{1}{4} = \qquad\qquad \frac{3}{7} \div \frac{4}{9} =$$

$$\frac{4}{5} \div \frac{5}{6} = \qquad\qquad \frac{1}{4} \div \frac{3}{10} =$$

$$\frac{2}{5} \div \frac{1}{3} = \qquad\qquad \frac{1}{8} \div \frac{9}{10} =$$

Ratio and proportion

A rat has 7 babies every 4 months.
How many babies does the rat have in one year?   21

In a class, there are 2 girls for every 3 boys.
There are 10 girls. How many boys are there?

In a week, a dog eats 4 cans of dog food with 7 biscuits.
How many biscuits are needed for 24 cans?

A cook uses 6 apples with 300 g flour to make an apple
crumble. How many apples are needed with 1.5 kg
of flour?

In a bathroom, a black tile is used for every 5 white tiles.
How many black tiles are needed for 60 white tiles?

An account earns £2.50 interest for every £10 000 saved.
How much interest is earned on £150 000?

A rectangle is drawn with length 5 cm x width 8 cm.
If it is drawn 4 times larger with length 20 cm, what is the
width?

A model of a building uses the scale 10 cm = 200 ft.
The model of the building is 75 cm high. What is the
actual height going to be?

Algebra

Work out this equation.

a + 5 = 7	10 − b = 4	a + 4 = 14 − 6
a + 5 (−5) = 7 (−5)	10 −b (+ b) = 4 (+ b)	a + 4 = 8
a = 2	10 (−4) = 4 + b (−4)	a + 4 (−4) = 8 (−4)
	b = 6	a = 4

Find value of each letter.

a + 6 = 24	b − 5 = 14
a + 28 = 42	b − 17 = 17
a + 17 = 25	b − 27 = 23
10 + y = 12	16 − x = 4
38 + y = 50	26 − x = 9
42 + y = 64	42 − x = 20

Solve these equations.

15 + a = 42 − 17	y + 13 = 7 × 5
100 − b = 72 + 14	x − 42 = 96 ÷ 8
63 + a = 9 × 9	21 − y = 40 − 25

Write equations for these problems and then solve them.

Laura had a bookcase overloaded with books.
She gave 24 to a school fair. She had 36 left.
How many books did she have to begin with?

Dan collected comics. He was given a set
of 12 for his birthday. He now had 64 in his
collection. How many comics did he
have before his birthday?

Decimal addition

Write the answer to each sum.

| 491.83 | 964.71 | 302.04 | 306.25 |
| + 137.84 | + 321.26 | + 204.99 | + 844.24 |

| 471.93 | 842.01 | 675.82 | 137.82 |
| + 755.26 | + 711.84 | + 105.23 | + 399.71 |

| 465.24 | 178.93 | 184.74 | 443.27 |
| + 605.27 | + 599.41 | + 372.81 | + 705.99 |

| 563.23 | 703.95 | 825.36 | 529.33 |
| + 413.98 | + 685.11 | + 249.85 | + 482.56 |

Write the answer to each sum.

421.79 + 136.25 =   192.31 + 241.73 =

558.32 + 137.94 =   501.84 + 361.93 =

227.66 + 142.07 =   275.31 + 239.33 =

153.31 + 189.02 =   491.44 + 105.37 =

253.71 + 562.41 =   829.25 + 163.74 =

206

Problems with negative numbers

What is the difference in temperature between Boston and Barcelona?

11°C

By how much would the temperature have to go
up in Boston to be the same as London?

9°C

City	Temperature
Boston	−9°C
Barcelona	2°C
London	0°C

City	Temperature
Athens	2°C
New York	−6°C
Tokyo	1°C

City	Temperature
Warsaw	−7°C
Zurich	−12°C
Rome	5°C

By how much is Athens warmer than Warsaw?

If the temperature went up by 5°C, what would it be in:

New York   Zurich   Warsaw

If the temperature went down by 6°C, what would it be in:

Tokyo   Rome   Athens

The temperature outside is −11°C. If it rises by 7°C,
what is the new temperature?

The temperature inside a shelter is 5°C.
The temperature outside is 12°C lower.
What is the temperature outside?

The frozen food compartments in a
supermarket are kept at a constant
temperature of −7°C. During a power cut
the temperature rises to 10°C.
By how much has the temperature risen?

The temperature at midnight is −8°C.
At midday it is 15°C higher.
What is the temperature at midday?

Real life problems

A man walks 18.34 km on Saturday and 16.57 km on Sunday.
How far did he walk that weekend?

34.91 km

How much further did he walk on Saturday?

1.77 km

```
   18.34
 + 16.57
   34.91
   1   1
     7 1 21
   18.34
 - 16.57
    1.77
```

A rectangular field measures 103.7 m by 96.5 m. How long is the perimeter of the field?

When Joe and Kerry stand on a weighing machine it reads 136.53 kg. When Joe steps off, it reads 68.76 kg. How much does Joe weigh?

A rectangular room has an area of 32.58 m². When a carpet is put down there is still 7.99 m² of floor showing. What is the area of the carpet?

A brother and sister's combined height is 3.27 m. If the sister is 1.59 m tall, how tall is the brother?

A country has 4 motorways, the MA which is 1 246 km long, the MB which is 339 km long, the MC which is 1 573 km long, and the MD which is 48 km long. How much motorway does the country have in total?

Jenny's aquarium holds 25.56 litres of water. She buys a new one which holds 32 litres. How much extra water do her fish have?

Simple use of brackets

Work out these calculations.

$(4 + 6) - (2 + 1) =$ $10 - 3 = 7$

$(2 \times 5) + (10 - 4) =$ $10 + 6 = 16$

Work out the brackets first.

Work out these calculations.

$(5 + 3) \quad + \quad (6 - 2) =$ $(3 - 1) \quad + \quad (12 - 1) =$

$(6 - 1) \quad - \quad (1 + 2) =$ $(9 + 5) \quad - \quad (3 + 6) =$

$(8 + 3) \quad + \quad (12 - 2) =$ $(14 + 12) - \quad (9 + 4) =$

$(7 - 2) \quad + \quad (4 + 5) =$ $(9 - 3) \quad - \quad (4 + 2) =$

Now try these longer calculations.

$(5 + 9) \quad + \quad (12 - 2) \quad - \quad (4 + 3) \quad =$

$(10 + 5) \quad - \quad (2 + 4) \quad + \quad (9 + 6) \quad =$

$(19 + 4) \quad - \quad (3 + 2) \quad - \quad (2 + 1) \quad =$

$(24 - 5) \quad - \quad (3 + 7) \quad - \quad (5 - 2) \quad =$

$(15 + 3) \quad + \quad (7 - 2) \quad - \quad (5 + 7) \quad =$

Now try these. Be careful, the brackets now have multiplication calculations.

$(2 \times 3) \quad + \quad (5 \times 2) \quad =$ $(3 \times 4) \quad - \quad (2 \times 2) \quad =$

$(7 \times 2) \quad + \quad (3 \times 3) \quad =$ $(5 \times 4) \quad - \quad (3 \times 2) \quad =$

$(6 \times 4) \quad - \quad (4 \times 3) \quad =$ $(9 \times 5) \quad - \quad (4 \times 6) \quad =$

$(12 \times 4) \quad - \quad (8 \times 3) \quad =$ $(7 \times 4) \quad - \quad (8 \times 2) \quad =$

If the answer is 24, which of these calculations gives the correct answer? Write the letter in the box.

a $(3 + 5) + \quad (3 \times 1)$ c $(3 \times 5) + \quad (3 \times 3)$ e $(5 \times 7) - \quad (2 \times 5)$

b $(3 \times 5) + \quad (3 \times 2)$ d $(2 \times 5) + \quad (2 \times 6)$ f $(6 + 7) + \quad (12 - 2)$

Multiplying decimals

Work out these calculations.

1.456	1.456	1.456	1.456
x 10	x 20	x 3	x 23
14.56	29.12	4.368	29.120
			+ 4.368
			33.488

Multiply these numbers.

2.567	4.687	8.924	3.963
x 10	x 10	x 100	x 100

12.892	7.689	9.578	15.432
x 100	x 1000	x 1000	x 1000

Multiply these numbers.

0.456	0.351	1.764	14.23
x 2	x 4	x 8	x 3

0.859	1.034	8.049	69.23
x 7	x 6	x 5	x 3

2.836	0.765	5.218	62.73
x 12	x 18	x 30	x 45

1.873	20.72	708.7	8.302
x 60	x 21	x 15	x 40

Division by units

47÷2 can be written in two ways:

$$23\frac{1}{2}$$ or $$23.5$$

2 | 47   2 | 47.0

Write the answers to these calculations with fraction remainders (amounts left over).

2 | 17   4 | 19   3 | 16   4 | 37

3 | 29   2 | 45   5 | 87   5 | 49

4 | 73   3 | 35   4 | 93   5 | 69

Write the answers to these calculations with decimal remainders.

2 | 73   2 | 85   2 | 39   4 | 59

4 | 71   4 | 83   5 | 29   5 | 47

5 | 24   2 | 77   4 | 38   5 | 93

Write the answers to these calculations choosing decimal or fraction remainders.

2 | 37   2 | 59   4 | 93   4 | 51

5 | 21   2 | 83   4 | 31   5 | 63

Division of 3-digit decimal numbers

Work out these division calculations.

$$5 \overline{\smash{)}\,9.95} = \overset{1.99}{\underset{44}{}}$$

$$6 \overline{\smash{)}\,9.66} = \overset{1.61}{\underset{3}{}}$$

Work out these division calculations.

$5 \overline{\smash{)}\,8.15}$ $5 \overline{\smash{)}\,9.25}$ $5 \overline{\smash{)}\,6.35}$ $6 \overline{\smash{)}\,6.36}$

$6 \overline{\smash{)}\,2.16}$ $7 \overline{\smash{)}\,8.82}$ $7 \overline{\smash{)}\,4.83}$ $8 \overline{\smash{)}\,5.92}$

$8 \overline{\smash{)}\,8.72}$ $9 \overline{\smash{)}\,8.19}$ $9 \overline{\smash{)}\,5.67}$ $6 \overline{\smash{)}\,9.12}$

$6 \overline{\smash{)}\,5.94}$ $8 \overline{\smash{)}\,8.48}$ $7 \overline{\smash{)}\,2.66}$ $7 \overline{\smash{)}\,9.45}$

$9 \overline{\smash{)}\,7.56}$ $8 \overline{\smash{)}\,9.44}$ $7 \overline{\smash{)}\,4.27}$ $7 \overline{\smash{)}\,9.17}$

Write the answer in the box.

What is 8.82 divided by 9?

What is 8.22 divided by 6?

Share 3.78 equally among 6

Find $\frac{1}{8}$ of 9.28

Find $\frac{1}{9}$ of 5.85

What is 3.12 divided by 8?

Work out the answer to each calculation.

Sammy spends £2.85 a week on his bus fares to school. How much is his bus fare each day?

A fence is 9.48 metres long. If it is made up of 6 panels, how long is each panel?

Real life problems

A family is driving 120 km to visit friends. If they have already driven 30% of the distance, how far have they travelled?

$$\frac{120}{100} \times 30 =$$ 36 km

Mr Chang gets a £500 bonus from his firm.
He puts 40% in the bank and spends the rest.
How much does he put in the bank?

How much does he spend?

 A school has 300 children. 55% of them are girls. How many boys are there in the school?

In a spelling test of 80 words Sinead gets 75% right. How many does she get wrong?

 A man wins £5 000 on the lottery. If he gives 25% to charity, how much does he keep for himself?

A team of 5 people works from 09:00 until 17:00 every day. If they each have an hour's lunch break, how many hours do they work altogether between Monday and Friday?

A train leaves at 08:47 and arrives at 16:29.
How long does the journey take?

Reading from scales

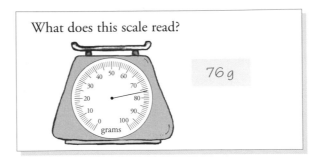

What does this scale read?

76 g

What do these scales read?

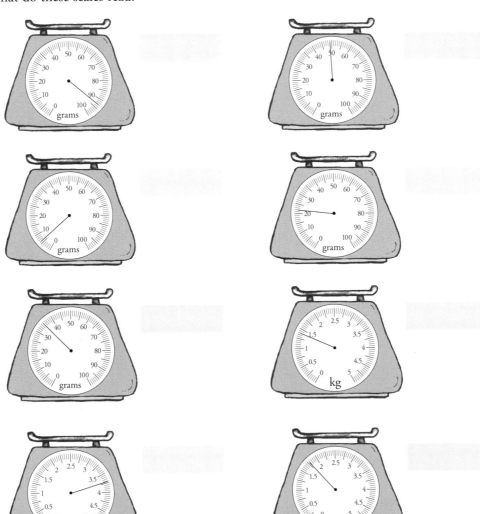

Mean, median, and mode

Sian throws a dice 7 times. Here are her results:

4, 2, 1, 2, 4, 2, 6

What is the mean? $(4 + 2 + 1 + 2 + 4 + 2 + 6) \div 7 = 3$

What is the median?   Put the numbers in order of size and find the middle number, e.g., 1, 2, 2, 2, 4, 4, 6.

The median is 2.

What is the mode?   The most common result, which is 2.

A school football team scores the following number of goals in their first 9 matches:
2, 2, 1, 3, 2, 1, 2, 4, 1

What is the mean score?

What is the median score?

Write down the mode for their results.

The ages of a local hockey team were:
17, 15, 16, 19, 17, 19, 22, 17, 18, 21, 17

What is the mean of their ages?

What is their median age?

Write down the mode for their ages.

The results of Susan's last 11 spelling tests were:
15, 12, 15, 17, 11, 16, 19, 11, 3, 11, 13

What is the mean of her scores?

What is her median score?

Write down the mode for her scores.

Multiplying decimals

Work out these calculations.

4.6	3.9	8.4
× 3	× 5	× 8
13.8	19.5	67.2
1	4	3

Work out these calculations.

4.7	9.1	5.8	1.7	5.1
× 3	× 3	× 3	× 2	× 2

7.4	3.6	6.5	4.2	3.8
× 2	× 4	× 4	× 2	× 2

4.2	4.7	1.8	3.4	3.7
× 4	× 4	× 5	× 5	× 5

2.5	2.4	5.3	7.2	5.1
× 5	× 6	× 7	× 8	× 9

7.9	8.6	8.8	7.5	9.9
× 9	× 9	× 8	× 8	× 6

6.8	5.7	6.9	7.5	8.4
× 7	× 6	× 7	× 9	× 9

7.3	2.8	3.8	7.7	9.4
× 8	× 7	× 8	× 7	× 9

Multiplying decimals

Work out these calculations.

37.5	26.2	65.3
× 2	× 5	× 9
75.0	131.0	587.7
1 1	3 1	4 2

Work out these calculations.

53.3	93.2	51.4	34.6	35.2
× 2	× 2	× 2	× 3	× 3

46.5	25.8	16.4	47.1	37.4
× 4	× 4	× 3	× 5	× 5

12.4	46.3	17.5	36.5	72.4
× 5	× 5	× 6	× 6	× 7

37.5	20.3	73.4	92.6	47.9
× 7	× 7	× 7	× 6	× 6

53.9	75.6	28.8	79.4	99.9
× 8	× 8	× 8	× 8	× 9

37.9	14.8	35.4	46.8	27.2
× 9	× 9	× 9	× 8	× 7

39.5	84.2	68.5	73.2	47.6
× 6	× 9	× 8	× 9	× 6

Real life problems

In a class of 30 children 6 children are painting.
What percentage of children are painting?
$\frac{6}{30}$ of the children are painting and
to change a fraction to a percentage
we multiply by 100.

20%

$$\frac{6}{30} \times 100 = 20$$

40% of a class is made up of girls. If there are
12 girls, how many children are in the class?
If 12 girls are 40% of the class, we
divide 12 by 40 to find 1%.
Then we multiply by 100 to find 100%.

30 children

$$\frac{12}{40} \times 100 = 30$$

A shop has 60 books by a new author. If it sells 45
of the books what percentage does it sell?

A school disco sells 65% of its tickets. If it had
120 tickets to start with, how many has it sold?

200 people go on a school trip. If 14% are adults,
how many children go on the trip?

A shop sells 150 T-shirts but 12 are returned
because they are faulty. What percentage of
the T-shirts was faulty?

A year group of 120 children are asked their
favourite colours.

15% like red. How many children like red?

20% like green. How many children like green?

30% like yellow. How many children like yellow?

35% like blue. How many children like blue?

Real life problems

Deborah's school bag weighs 4.67 kg.
Asha's weighs 3.98 kg. How much more does
Deborah's weigh than Asha's?

$$\begin{array}{r} 3^{\ 1}51 \\ 4.\cancel{6}7 \\ -3.98 \\ \hline 0.69 \end{array}$$

       0.69 kg

What is the total weight of the two bags?

$$\begin{array}{r} 4.67 \\ +3.98 \\ \hline 8.65 \\ \hline {\scriptstyle 1\ 1} \end{array}$$

       8.65 kg

A man wants to fit a new door. If the door frame is
2m 5cm high and the new door is 2.09 m long,
how much will he have to cut off the door?

Bert earns £14 632 a year, George earns
£24 321 a year, and Horace earns £12 971
a year. How much do they earn altogether?

How much more than Bert
does George earn?

How much more than Horace does Bert
earn?

How much more than Horace does
George earn?

A lift says 'Maximum weight 270 kg'. If four people get in
weighing 72.93 kg, 47.81 kg, 85.99 kg, and 79.36 kg, by
how much are they overloading the lift?

Fraction problems

Find $\frac{3}{5}$ of £30.00.

| £30.00 ÷ 5 = £6.00 ($\frac{1}{5}$) |
| £6.00 x 3 = £18.00 ($\frac{3}{5}$) |
| $\frac{3}{5}$ of £30 is £18 |

Find $\frac{7}{10}$ of 60 cm.

| 60 cm ÷ 10 = 6 cm ($\frac{1}{10}$) |
| 6 cm x 7 = 42 cm ($\frac{7}{10}$) |
| $\frac{7}{10}$ of 60 cm is 42 cm |

Find $\frac{3}{5}$ of these amounts.

40 cm

£50

£10.50

80 m

75 g

45 kg

Find $\frac{7}{10}$ of these amounts.

48 m

£98.00

75 km

Find $\frac{2}{3}$ of these amounts.

48 cm

120 kg

£24.00

220

Finding percentages

Find 30% of 140.

(Divide by 100 to find 1% and then multiply by 30 to find 30%.) $\frac{140}{100} \times 30 = 42$

Find 12% of 75. $\frac{75^3}{100_4}_1 \times 12^3 = 9$

Find 30% of these numbers.

620   240

80   160

Find 60% of these numbers.

60   100

160   580

Find 45% of these amounts.

80 g   40 cm

240 ml   600 km

Find 12% of these amounts.

£150   £600

125 m   775 m

More algebra

Work out this equation.

$10 - a = a$
$10 - a\,(+a) = a\,(+a)$
$10 = 2a$
$10\,(\div 2) = 2a\,(\div 2)$
$a = 5$

$3b + 15 = 12 * 6$
$3b + 15\,(-15) = 72\,(-15)$
$3b = 57$
$3b\,(\div 3) = 57\,(\div 3)$
$b = 19$

$27 \div c = 9$
$27 \div c\,(\times c) = 9\,(\times c)$
$27 = 9c$
$27\,(\div 9) = 9c\,(\div 9)$
$3 = c$

Find value of each letter.

$5a = 25$

$a = 36 - a$

$6a = 42$

$3y + 8 = 20$

$6y - 16 = 38$

$42 - 5y = 22$

$15 \div c = 5$

$32 \div c = 8$

$56 \div c = 7$

$d \div 4 = 7$

$d \div 9 = 5$

$d \div 11 = 10$

Solve these equations.

$56 - a = 26 + 2a$

$2b + 16 = (12 \times 3) - 2$

$4y - 27 = 72 \div 8$

$48 \div d = 7 + 5$

$17 + c = 26 - 2c$

$4e + 45 = 35 + 6e$

Write equations for these problems and then solve them.

Isla bought two packets of biscuits and a 20 pence bunch of bananas. The total cost was 80 pence. How much is one pack of biscuits?

Jodie invited 48 guests to her New Year party. 10 people couldn't make it and half of the rest were going to arrive late. How many were going to be on time?

Multiplication by tens and units

Work out the answer to each calculation.

```
    527              834
  x  76            x  58
   36 890           41 700
    1 4              1 2
    3 162            6 672
      1 4              2 3
   40 052           48 372
    11 1              1
```

Work out the answer to each calculation.

```
    426              895              632              778
  x  84            x  65            x  39            x  49
  _____          _____          _____          _____

  _____          _____          _____          _____
```

```
    597              994              632              747
  x  46            x  37            x  64            x  75
  _____          _____          _____          _____

  _____          _____          _____          _____
```

```
    428              147              236              145
  x  95            x  62            x  87            x  33
  _____          _____          _____          _____

  _____          _____          _____          _____
```

```
    346              529              485              763
  x  85            x  72            x  29            x  84
  _____          _____          _____          _____

  _____          _____          _____          _____
```

Naming parts of a circle

Label the part of this circle.

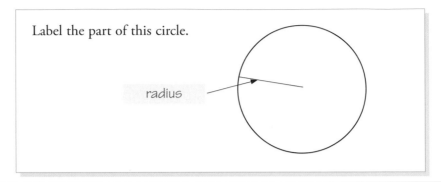

radius

Choose from the following words to label these circles:
radius, diameter, centre, arc, sector, quadrant

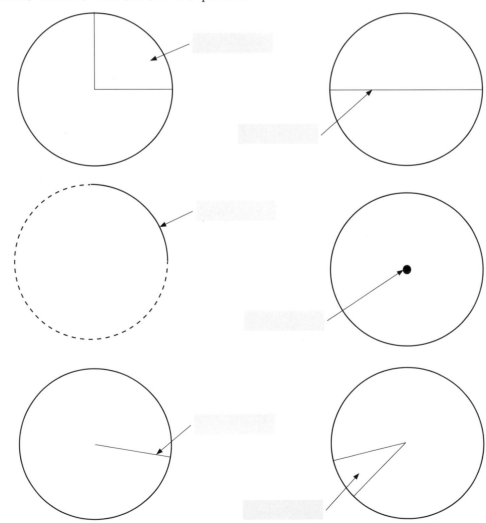

Area of right-angled triangles

Find the area of this right-angled triangle.

Because the area of this triangle is half the area of the rectangle shown, we can find the area of the rectangle and then divide it by two to find the area of the triangle.
So the area = (8 cm * 4 cm) ÷ 2
= 32 ÷ 2 = 16 cm²

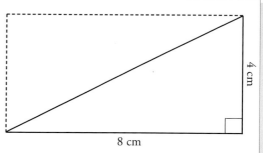

Area = 16 cm²

Find the areas of these right-angled triangles.

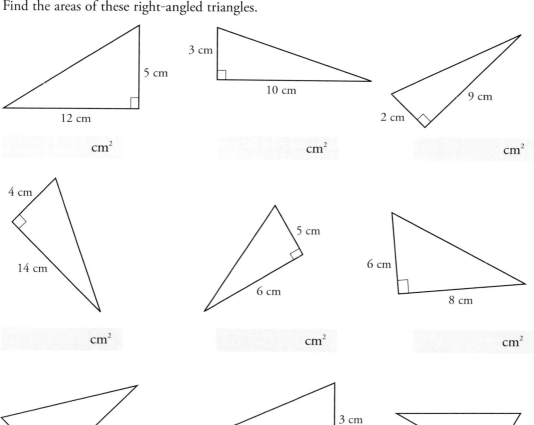

5 cm
12 cm

cm²

3 cm
10 cm

cm²

9 cm
2 cm

cm²

4 cm
14 cm

cm²

5 cm
6 cm

cm²

6 cm
8 cm

cm²

12 cm
6 cm

cm²

3 cm
20 cm

cm²

7 cm   4 cm

cm²

Cubes of small numbers

2^3 means:

$2 \times 2 \times 2 = 8$

Volume is the space inside a 3D shape.

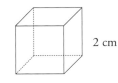

2 cm

What is the volume of this cube?

$2 \times 2 \times 2 = 8$ cm^3

You find the volume of a cube in the same way as working out the cube of a number.

Use extra paper here if you need to. What is...

3^3

4^3

6^3

5^3

1^3

2^3

What are the volumes of these cubes?

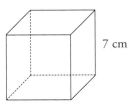

7 cm

cm^3

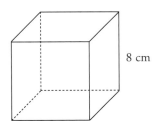

8 cm

cm^3

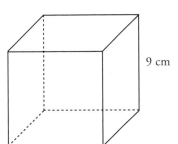

9 cm

cm^3

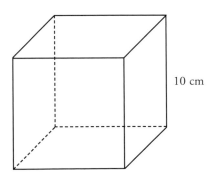

10 cm

cm^3

Cubes of larger numbers

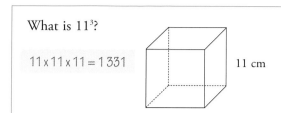

What is 11^3?

$11 \times 11 \times 11 = 1331$

11 cm

What is the volume of this cube?

$11 \times 11 \times 11 = 1331 \text{ cm}^3$

You find the volume of a cube in the same way as working out the cube of a number.

Use extra paper here if you need to. What is...

12^3 15^3

20^3 13^3

19^3 50^3

25^3 100^3

What are the volumes of these cubes?

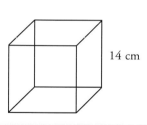

14 cm

cm^3

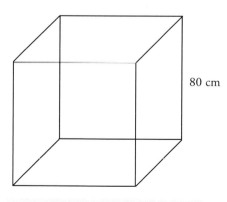

80 cm

cm^3

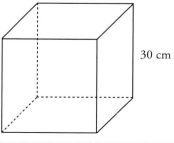

30 cm

cm^3

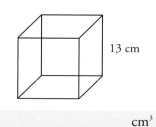

13 cm

cm^3

Nets of 3D shapes

For which 3D shape is this the net?

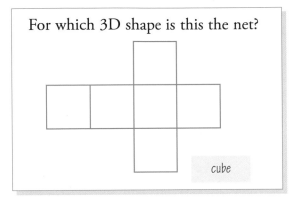

cube

For which 3D shapes are these the nets?

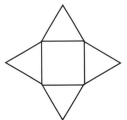

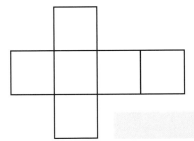

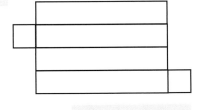

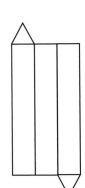

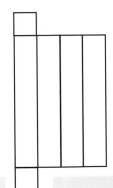

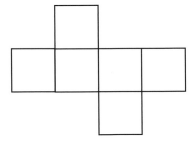

Nets of simple shapes

Sketch the net of this cuboid.

Sketch the nets of these shapes.

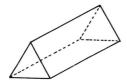

Triangular prism

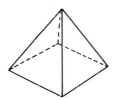

Square-based pyramid

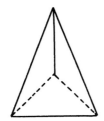

Triangular-based pyramid

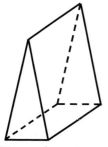

Triangular prism

Drawing angles including reflex

Acute angles are between 0° and 90°.   Obtuse angles are between 90° and 180°.

When you get to 180°
you have a straight line.

Reflex angles are bigger
than 180° and less than 360°.

Because reflex angles are bigger than 180°
you may find it easier to use a circular protractor in order to draw them.

Use a protractor to draw these angles. Remember to mark the angle you have drawn.

150°	135°

210°	350°

10°	20°

Drawing more angles including reflex

Draw these angles. Remember to mark the angle you have drawn.

275°

65°

330°

35°

25°

345°

165°

5°

Drawing 2D shapes

Congruent shapes are shapes that have angles and sides of exactly the same size.

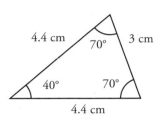 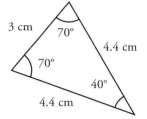

These shapes are congruent because they can be fitted exactly on top of each other.

Measure the angles and sides of these shapes and draw a congruent shape next to each one.

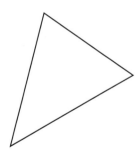 

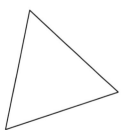 

Coordinates

Write the coordinates of:

A   (2, 4)

B   (3, 1)

C   (1, 1)

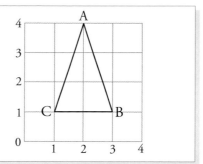

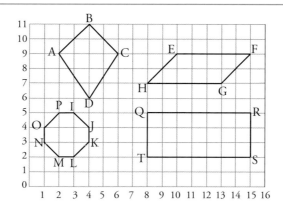

Write the coordinates of:

A	B	C	D	E
F	G	H	I	J
K	L	M	N	O
P	Q	R	S	T

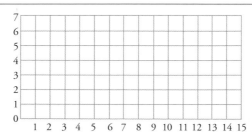

Plot these points on the grid, and join them up in the right order.
(0, 1) (1, 3) (3, 3) (5, 1) (0, 1). What shape does this make?

(3, 6) (4, 7) (9, 2) (8, 1) (3, 6). What shape does this make?

(11, 3) (13, 5) (15, 3) (13, 1) (11, 3). What shape does this make?

p28 — Reading a text

Read this **text**, then answer the questions in full sentences.

The Voice of Nature

An Aboriginal myth from southern Australia relates how, in the beginning, the voice of the Ancestor spoke each day from a great gum tree, and the tribe gathered around to listen. But as time went by the people grew weary of hearing his words of wisdom. One by one they turned their backs on the voice to pursue their own pleasures, and a vast silence settled over the whole of the land and the sea. There was no wind and the tides were still, no birds sang, and the earth seemed to be dying.

The tribe soon wearied of the pleasures of their own making and began to be afraid and lonely. They returned to the great tree again and again, hoping to hear the words that would ease their misery. And one day the voice of their Ancestor spoke again.

He told them it was the last time his voice would be heard, but that he would give them a sign. The great tree split open, a huge tongue of light came down into its trunk, and then it closed up again.

Since that time the Aboriginals have known that the voice of their Ancestor exists in all things, and speaks to them through every part of nature.

From *Dreamtime Heritage* by A. & M. J. Roberts

Why did the tribe traditionally gather around the great gum tree?
The tribe used to gather around the great gum tree to hear the Ancestor speak.

Why did the people abandon this custom (stop going to the tree)?
They abandoned this custom because they grew weary of hearing the Ancestor's words of wisdom.

What happened to the natural world when the people broke this tradition?
When people broke this tradition, there was no wind or tides, no birds sang, and and the earth seemed to be dying.

What feelings made the people return to the tree?
Feelings of fear and loneliness made people return to the tree.

p29 — Reading and understanding

Reread the **text** on page 28, then answer the following questions in full sentences.

What is an **ancestor**? D
An ancestor is someone from whom a person is descended.

Describe the sign given to the people by the Ancestor. Explain the meaning of the sign.
The great tree split open, a huge tongue of light came down into its trunk, and then it closed up again. This was a sign that the Ancestor is present in all things and speaks to the people through every part of nature.

The Australian gum tree has a **scientific** name. Use **reference books** or a **computer** to find out what it is, and write it here.
Eucalyptus

Explain the word **tribe**. What do we mean by **tribal society**? D
A tribe is a group of people with common ancestors. Tribal society is a society organised around the culture and rules of a tribe.

What evidence can you find in the text to suggest that **nature** was important to the people? Can you explain why this was?
The people felt afraid and lonely when the earth seemed to be dying. They gathered round the gum tree every day to listen to their Ancestor.

Use a **dictionary** to find out what the saying "up a gum tree" means. D
The saying "up a gum tree" means to be in a very awkward or difficult position.

What does this passage make you feel?
Which words make you feel like this?

Answers may vary

Note: D means to use a dictionary for these practice pages.
In the actual test, children will not be able to use a dictionary.

p30 — A traditional story

Read this **story** from India about a tree, and answer the questions in full sentences. The writer explains that, as a child, she often heard this story told on a special day in August – the Day for Brothers – when "all sisters in India pray that no harm comes to their brothers".

The Mango Tree (Part One)

In a small town, there was a small house in which lived a young man, his wife, and the young man's sister. This small house had a small garden at the back in which grew a small mango tree. One day the young man's wife came to him and said, "Look here, I'm fed up with our situation. Your sister …"

"Have you come here to complain about my sister again?"

"What can I do? I know it's quite useless … My complaints fall on deaf ears, anyway … I'm just … so angry with your sister. I get up early in the morning, draw water from the well, light the fire in the kitchen, cook breakfast, wash and scrub pots …"

"Don't go on," said the brother. "I've heard it all before."

"And what does your lazy sister do all day? Nothing … nothing … she lolls about in the garden, watering her mango tree, talking to it, clearing away dead leaves, and feeding it manure and mulch …"

"That isn't all she does. She comes in and talks to me. Just an hour ago, she was playing chess with me."

"Just because she adores you, doesn't mean you should ignore her faults. You must tell her to leave that … silly mango tree alone, and come and help me with the housework. I think she needs to get married. That might teach her to be more responsible."

Since the sister was of marriageable age, the brother could not really object. He knew though, that he would miss her very, very much.

A marriage was planned.

Why did the young man's wife complain to him?
She complained because the young man's sister did nothing all day except care for the mango tree.

Why did the wife think the sister should marry?
The sister should marry as this might teach her to be more responsible.

p31

Now read part two of the **story** that began on page 30, then answer the questions.

The Mango Tree (Part Two)

When all the ceremonies were over, and the sister was about to leave with her groom to lead a new life in a new town, she turned to her sister-in-law and said, "Dearest sister-in-law, I'm going to miss my mango tree so much. Would you please do me a great favour and look after it for me? Please water it well and clear the weeds that grow in its shadow."

"Oh, well, yes, yes," answered the sister-in-law.

Once the sister had left, the sister-in-law turned to her husband and yelled, "Did you hear that? Did *you* hear that? Did you hear your selfish sister? She didn't say that she was going to miss you. She didn't say that she was going to miss me. She *did* say that she was going to miss her mango tree!" She decided then that she was going to ignore the mango tree. The mango tree irritated her just as much as her husband's sister had. Now she could be rid of both.

As the days passed, the unwatered, uncared for mango tree started drying up and its leaves began to fall.

At the same time, the brother, who had been a strong, robust and healthy young man, began to lose his appetite and get thinner and weaker.

One day, a letter arrived. It was from the sister and said, "Dearest brother and sister-in-law. I hope all is well and that my tree is green, and that my brother is in good health."

The remaining leaves of the mango tree were quite yellow by this time, but the sister-in-law wrote back, "Dearest sister. Your tree is fine, but your brother has not been feeling so good."

Soon another letter arrived from the sister. "Are you sure my tree is green? And how is my brother?"

Why did the young man's wife object when his sister said that she would miss her mango tree?
The man's wife felt that his sister cared more about the tree than she cared about them.

Explain why the young man's wife neglected the tree.
She neglected the tree because she was annoyed with her sister-in-law and the fuss she had made of the tree.

Which words in the story so far would you use in your own writing, and why?

Answers may vary

Understanding poetry

Read this **poem** aloud.

The Rabbit

We are going to see the rabbit.
We are going to see the rabbit.
Which rabbit, people say?
Which rabbit, ask the children?
Which rabbit?
The only rabbit,
The only rabbit in England,
Sitting behind a barbed-wire fence
Under the floodlights, neon lights,
Sodium lights,
Nibbling grass
On the only patch of grass
In England, in England
(Except the grass by the hoardings
Which doesn't count.)
We are going to see the rabbit
And we must be there on time.

First we shall go by escalator,
Then we shall go by underground,
And then we shall go by motorway
And then by helicopterway,
And the last ten yards we shall have to go
On foot.

And now we are going
All the way to see the rabbit,
We are nearly there,
We are longing to see it,
And so is the crowd
Which is here in thousands
With mounted policemen
And big loudspeakers
And bands and banners,
And everyone has come a long way.
But soon we shall see it
Sitting and nibbling
The blades of grass
On the only patch of grass
In – but something has gone wrong!
Why is everyone so angry,
Why is everyone jostling
And slanging and complaining?

The rabbit has gone,
Yes, the rabbit has gone.
He has actually burrowed down into the
    earth
And made himself a warren, under the earth,
Despite all these people.
And what shall we do?
What *can* we do?

It is all a pity, you must be disappointed,
Go home and do something else for today,
Go home again, go home for today.
For you cannot hear the rabbit, under the earth,
Remarking rather sadly to himself, by himself,
As he rests in his warren, under the earth:
'It won't be long, they are bound to come,
They are bound to come and find me, even here.'

Alan Brownjohn

Reading and understanding

Reread the **poem** on page 32, then answer the following questions in full sentences.

Is this **poem** about the past, the present or the future? What evidence is there in the poem for your answer?
I can tell this poem is about the future because there is only one patch of grass
left in England and only one rabbit.

Why do you think that this is the only rabbit on the only patch of grass?
I think there is no room left for grass and so the rabbits have died out
because they had nothing to eat.

What is a hoarding? D
A hoarding is a large board on the side of the road that displays advertisements.

Five ways of travelling are mentioned in the **poem**. What are they? Which is least harmful to the environment?
The five methods of transport in the poem are escalator, underground, motorway,
helicopter and on foot. On foot is the least harmful.

Find the **noun** that names the rabbit's home, then write another word for a rabbit's home. **Remember**: A **noun** is a naming word. D
In the poem the rabbit's home is called a warren. It can also be called a burrow.

Can you name the wild animals that live in a **sett**, an **earth** and a **holt**. D
A badger lives in a sett, a fox lives in an earth and an otter lives in a holt.

Why is the rabbit sad?
The rabbit is sad because he is alone and because he can't escape the crowds
of people.

In some places rabbits are regarded as pests. What does this mean?
In some places, rabbits eat crops that people have grown.

Letter of complaint

Read this **letter**, then answer in full sentences the questions that follow.

Parkview,
Green Lane,
Greenford
11th April

The Chairman,
Greenford Council

Dear Sir,

 I am writing to complain about the state of the waste ground, formerly known as Greenford Park, which can be seen from the front of my house.
 I use the word "waste" deliberately as this, in truth, is what it has become.
 Are we, as local residents, expected to suffer the misuse and probable ruination of this once useful, attractive amenity without expressing our feelings?
 For the last month, I have noted the following thoughtless actions that have contributed to its present condition:

• the casual dropping of litter in the form of cans, fast-food packaging, etc.,
• the deliberate dumping of an old mattress,
• damage to the few remaining trees and wild plants from vehicles either crossing the area or parking on it,
• the careless behaviour of dog owners who allow their pets to foul the area without any attempt to clear up the mess that remains, thus endangering public health.

 Added to these obvious forms of pollution, there is the noise from portable "music-making" devices in fine weather, which must contribute to the disappearance of the rabbits, badgers and other species from this once beautifully unspoilt wild area.
 In these days of conservation and "green" awareness, I should have thought that our council might leap at the chance to create an area that would promote the preservation of plants and wildlife.

Yours faithfully,
Mr I. M. Wild

What is the writer's reason for writing? In which paragraph does he first state his reason?
The writer's reason for writing is to complain about the state of Greenford
Park. He states this in paragraph 1.

Why does Mr Wild use inverted commas around the word "music-making"?
Mr Wild uses inverted commas around 'music-making' because he does not
think these machines make real music.

Reading and understanding

Answer the following questions about the **letter** on page 34.

How does the writer suggest that he is writing on behalf of everyone living in Greenford?
The writer suggests he is writing on behalf of everyone living in Greenford by
using the words "we" and "the local residents".

How does the writer make clear his four main complaints? What are they?
The writer makes his complaints clear by listing them with bullet points.
He complains about litter, dumping, damage to trees and plants by vehicles
and fouling by pets.

Why does Mr Wild use words such as **casual**, **deliberate**, **thoughtless** and **careless**?
Mr Wild uses these words to emphasise the selfishness of the people who
damage Greenford Park.

The writer is trying to persuade the council to do something. Which words or phrases suggest this?
The words "in these days of conservation and 'green' awareness I should have
thought that our council..." tell us the writer wants the council to help.

Is this just a **letter of complaint**, or does it make any suggestions for improvement? If so, what are they?
The writer suggests that the council makes the Park into an area that will
promote the preservation of plants and wildlife, but he does not say how.

A **rhetorical question** is used to make people think, and an answer is not usually expected. Can you find the **rhetorical question** in this **letter** and write it here?
Are we, as local residents, expected to suffer the misuse and probable ruination
of this once useful, attractive amenity without expressing our feelings?

Do you think this letter will be successful? Why do you think this?

Reading a classic novel

In the nineteenth century, some writers wanted their readers to understand more about the lives of others. In those days before television and the Internet, books were one of the most important ways of **persuading** people to think about the rest of the world.

In Chapters 5 and 17 of his novel *Hard Times*, Charles Dickens describes Coketown, an industrial city in the north of England. Read his description of Coketown in these **extracts**.

It was a town of red brick, or of brick that would have been red if the smoke and ashes had allowed it; … It was a town of machinery and tall chimneys, out of which interminable serpents of smoke trailed themselves for ever and ever, and never got uncoiled. It had a black canal in it, and a river that ran purple with ill-smelling dye, and vast piles of building full of windows where there was a rattling and a trembling all day long, and where the piston of the steam-engine worked monotonously up and down, like the head of an elephant in a state of melancholy madness. It contained several large streets all very like one another, and many small streets still more like one another, inhabited by people equally like one another, who all went in and out at the same hours, with the same sound upon the same pavements, to do the same work, and to whom every day was the same as yesterday and tomorrow, and every year the counterpart of the last and the next.

… The streets were hot and dusty on the summer day, and the sun was so bright that it even shone through the heavy vapour drooping over Coketown, and could not be looked at steadily. Stokers emerged from low underground doorways into factory yards, and sat on steps, and posts, and palings, wiping their swarthy visages, and contemplating coals. The whole town seemed to be frying in oil. There was a stifling smell of hot oil everywhere. The steam-engines shone with it, the dresses of the Hands were soiled with it, the mills throughout their many storeys oozed and trickled it … their inhabitants, wasting with heat, toiled languidly in the desert. But no temperature made the melancholy-mad elephants more mad or more sane. Their wearisome heads went up and down at the same rate in hot weather and cold, wet weather and dry, fair weather and foul. The measured motion of their shadows on the walls, was the substitute Coketown had to show for the shadows of rustling woods; while, for the summer hum of insects, it could offer, all the year round, from the dawn of Monday to the night of Saturday, the whirr of shafts and wheels.

Note: The extracts on pages 36 and 38 are being used to practise the reading skills, and may be harder than the actual SATs papers.

Reading and understanding

Answer these questions about the **extracts** on page 36.

Charles Dickens uses more detail than many modern writers would. Why do you think this is?
Unfamiliar scenes had to be described in detail because people did not have
TVs or videos showing pictures of them.

Dickens uses many long sentences and repeats words. What effect does this have on the reader?
It conveys the monotony of Coketown life and gives structure and rhythm
to the text, it is like the rhythm of machinery.

Find as many **adjectives** describing **colours**, **sounds** and **smells** as you can. Write them here.
Remember: An **adjective** is a describing word.
red, black, purple, ill-smelling, rattling, trembling, swarthy, stifling, rustling

Find a **metaphor** for smoke and write it here.
Remember: A writer uses a **metaphor** to describe something as if it were something else.
Interminable serpents

Find a **simile** for a steam-engine and write it here.
Remember: A **simile** is used to compare one thing with another to create an image in the reader's mind. It often includes the words **like** or **as**.
Like the head of an elephant in a state of melancholy madness

Here are some of the words that you may have found unfamiliar or difficult. Draw a line to match each one with its meaning. The first one has been done for you. D

interminable	very sad
monotonously	leaked slowly
melancholy	endless
counterpart	weakly
wearisome	same
stokers	in the same dull way
visage	furnace feeders
oozed	boring and tiring
languidly	face

Reading another classic novel

Charles Dickens also wrote *David Copperfield*, a novel about a man's life. As a young boy, David is treated harshly by his stepfather and bullied at school. At the age of ten, he is sent to London to work. Being clever and ambitious, he finds the work very boring. Here, the grown-up David Copperfield describes that particular period in his life.

… I became, at ten years old, a little labouring hind in the service of Murdstone and Grinby.

Murdstone and Grinby's warehouse was at the water side. It was down in Blackfriars … it was the last house at the bottom of a narrow street, curving down hill to the river, with some stairs at the end, where people took boats. It was a crazy old house with a wharf of its own, abutting on the water when the tide was in, and on the mud when the tide was out, and literally over-run with rats. Its panelled rooms, discoloured with the dirt and smoke of a hundred years, I dare say; its decaying floors and staircase, the squeaking and scuffling of the old grey rats down in the cellars; and the dirt and rottenness of the place; are things which, not of many years ago, in my mind, but of the present instant. They are all before me, just as they were in the evil hour when I went among them for the first time. …

Murdstone and Grinby's trade was among a good many kinds of people, but an important branch of it was the supply of wines and spirits to certain packet ships. … I think there were some among them that made voyages both to the East and West Indies. I know that a great many empty bottles were one of the consequences of this traffic, and that certain men and boys were employed to examine them against the light, and to reject those that were flawed, and to rinse and wash them. When the empty bottles ran short, there were labels to be pasted on full ones, or corks to be fitted to them, or seals to be put upon the corks, or finished bottles to be packed in casks. All this work was my work, and of the boys employed upon it I was one.

Name the **narrator** of this part of the story. D
David Copperfield

Explain the difference between a **narrator** and an **author**. D
The author is the person who writes the book and the
narrator is the character in the book who tells the story.

Reading and understanding

Answer these questions about the **extract** on page 38.

The third **paragraph** describes the kind of work that the men and boys did. Can you explain briefly what it was?
The men and boys inspected bottles, rinsed and washed them. They also pasted on
labels, fitted corks and seals, and packed the bottles.

Can you complete these **old words** and **phrases** from the extract? They match the meanings of the **modern words** given below. D

Modern word	Old word
next to	ab u t t i n g
rotting	d e c a y i n g
now	of the p r e s e n t i n s t a n t
journeys	vo y a g e s
a lot of	a g r e a t m a n y
results	co n s e q u e n c e s
damaged	f l a w e d
put on	put u p o n

A **hind** was a servant who lived in a house belonging to the master or mistress. Why is this word used in the first sentence?
The word "hind" was used in the first sentence so that the reader knows David
Copperfield's position in the company.

Do you think this **description** gives the reader a good idea of the way David felt? What words can you think of to describe his feelings about his life and work at this time?
The description gives a good idea of David's feelings. He felt the work was hard,
boring and depressing.

Fast fact-finding

Read the passage below.

Sky Colours

HAVE YOU EVER WONDERED why clear skies are sometimes deep blue and at other times almost white? Or why some sunsets are fiery red and others watery yellow? The reason is that the mixture of particles in the atmosphere is constantly changing. Every colour in the sky comes from the Sun. Sunlight is white, which means it is a mix of every colour in the rainbow. But as it passes through the atmosphere, gases, dust, ice crystals and water droplets split it into the various colours, bouncing some towards our eyes and absorbing others. The colours we see depend on which colours are reflected and which are absorbed. Clear skies are blue because gases in the air reflect mostly blue light from the Sun. The sky gets paler when extra dust or moisture reflects other colours, diluting the blue. Sunsets are yellow (or red, if the air is dusty) because the Sun's rays have to travel so far through the lower atmosphere that all the yellow light is absorbed.

From *How the Earth Works* by John Farndon

Underline all the **main points** in the paragraph above. Then answer these questions in full sentences.

What colour is sunlight?
Sunlight is white.

Why is the sky blue?
The sky is blue because gases in the air reflect mostly blue light from the Sun.

What do you notice about the first four words? Why do you think they are set out this way?
The first four words are in capital letters. They attract the reader's attention, drawing them into the text.

What kind of sentences introduce the passage?
The passage is introduced by questions.

Words such as **the reason is**, **because** and **which means** tell us that this piece of writing does more than simply list facts. What else does it do?
This piece of writing also explains how and why things happen.

Following instructions

Read the following piece of writing.

Experiment: Red and Blue Skies

It is not always easy to believe that all the colours in the sky come from the different way particles in the atmosphere reflect and absorb sunlight. But you can demonstrate it for yourself with this very simple experiment. The effects are quite subtle, and not always easy to see, so you need to conduct the experiment in a very dark room. Fill a straight glass with cold water, then add half a teaspoonful of milk. Now try shining the torch at the glass from different angles and watch how the colour of the milky water changes very slightly. Hold the torch close to the glass for a better effect. Add another half-teaspoonful of milk and repeat. Finally, add a full teaspoonful of milk, and try shining the torch at the glass from a variety of different angles.

From *How the Earth Works* by John Farndon

Read through the text again, underlining the actual **instructions**. On a separate sheet of paper, draw a **flow chart** that shows the **instructions** in the correct order.

Try the **experiment** yourself, then make **notes** under these headings.

Equipment/materials needed   straight glass of cold water, 2 teaspoons milk, teaspoon, torch

What I did   filled straight glass with cold water, added half a teaspoon of milk, shone torch at different angles

What I saw   *Answers may vary*

What I learnt from the experiment   *Answers may vary*

Non-fiction writing

FACTS

Non-fiction writing is based on facts and is different from stories, which come from an author's imagination. The following are all types of non-fiction writing: a retelling of real-life events; instructions; a technical explanation; an opinion or argument; a discussion; and a description of the characteristics of something. The chapters of non-fiction books can often be read in any order. Such books usually have a contents page, a glossary and an index.

Read this extract about the duck-billed platypus. Use the information to create an information leaflet. Give your piece of writing a heading and, if you want, use bullet points to highlight the animal's key characteristics.

All animals are different, but platypuses are particularly unusual animals. They look like a mixture of many other animals. They have flat tails, like beavers. They have thick fur that is well suited to water, like otters. They have bills and webbed feet, like ducks. Their webbed feet have claws, so they are able to dig and swim. Platypuses are also unusual because they are venomous mammals. A male platypus can sting other creatures to defend himself. Finally, platypuses are one of the very few mammals that lay eggs.

Answers may vary

Onomatopoeia

FACTS

Onomatopoeia is the formation of words that imitate the sound of the objects or actions to which they refer. For example; **crunch, hiccup, ha-ha, vroom** and animal noises, such as **moo, miaow** and **oink**, are all onomatopoeic words. It is a form of figurative language, like personification.

Read this poem. In the space provided below, list the onomatopoeic words the poet has used in the poem.

Clocks

Ding, Dong, Ding, Dong!
The grandfather clocks aren't wrong.
The clocks' hands turn around,
Standing tall above the ground.
Ding, Dong, Ding, Dong!

Beep, Beep, Beep, Beep!
Says the stopwatch after his sleep.
He will stop at your every word.
That beep is what everyone heard.
Beep, Beep, Beep, Beep!

Bong, Bong, Bong, Bong!
Big Ben sounds like a gong.
Towering tall over London city,
Making citizens look so tiny.
Bong, Bong, Bong, Bong!

Tick, Tick, Tick, Tick!
Chimes the ongoing wall clock.
It will stay ticking forever.
When will it stop? Never!

Craig Robson (age 11)

ding
dong   bong
beep   tick

p120

Silent consonants

FACTS

Some consonants are silent in the spelling of a word. They are written, but not pronounced. The secret silent consonants lurk where you cannot hear them. You will never know they are there, unless you know how to spell the word. For example: the **b** in **limb** and the **w** in **sword** are both silent consonants.

Look at the words in the word bank carefully. Then, fill in each silent-consonant box.

crumb   knee   doubt   wrist
    dough   who   high   right
knuckle   knot   neighbour   lamb
    write   wreck   knife   plumber

silent B
crumb
doubt
lamb
plumber

silent W
who
wrist
write
wreck

silent GH
dough
high
neighbour
right

silent K
knee
knuckle
knot
knife

p121

Root words

FACTS

A **root word** is usually a complete word in itself, such as **order** or **break**. You can, however, make a new word by adding a prefix or a suffix to a root word. For example: **dis** + **order** = **disorder** and **break** + **able** = **breakable**.

Remove the prefix or suffix from each of the words below to find the root word.

Word	Root word
misbehave	behave
sincerely	sincere
training	train
semicircle	circle
disagree	agree
intensify	intense
submarine	marine
disappear	appear
equipped	equip
lengthen	length
drinkable	drink
preschool	school

Now pick any two pairs of words from the chart above. Write four sentences, each including one of the words you picked.

answers may vary

p122

Prefixes

FACTS

A **prefix** is a group of letters added to the beginning of a root word to change its meaning. For example: **dis** + **approve** = **disapprove**.

Match each prefix to its meaning below. **Hint:** think about the words you know that use these prefixes and their meanings.

dis   again or back

de   reverses the meaning of the verb

mis   badly or wrongly

re   do the opposite of

Choose and write the correct prefix from the exercise above for each of these root words.

dis appear

re arrange

de frost

re cycle

de value

mis place

p123

Suffixes

FACTS

A **suffix** is a group of letters added to the end of a root word to change its meaning. For example: **walk** + **ing** = **walking**. Suffixes are not complete words and cannot be used on their own in a sentence.

Change the nouns and adjectives into verbs by adding one of these suffixes: **ate**, **ify**, **ise** or **en**.

Nouns/Adjectives	Verbs
standard	standardise
straight	straighten
note	notify
elastic	elasticate
deep	deepen
hyphen	hyphenate
apology	apologise
dead	deaden
pure	purify
loose	loosen
glory	glorify

What do you notice about the root words above ending in **y** and **e**?
The letters **y** and **e** are dropped when a suffix is added to the root words.

Choose two verbs from the exercise above and write sentences using them.

answers may vary

p124

Antonyms

An **antonym** is a word that has an opposite meaning to another word.

For example:

forget means the opposite of **remember**

Write an antonym for each of these words.

Answers may vary

strong	weak
first	last
near	far
youngest	oldest
clean	dirty
good	bad
question	answer
dark	light

Now try these. Read each complete word and then fill in the missing letters of the word beside it to make an antonym.

shorten — len _gth_ en

hope — des _pai_ r

antonym — sy _nony_ m

vertical — horiz _ont_ al

compulsory — volun _tar_ y

optional — nec _ess_ ary

p125

Antonyms: using a prefix

Antonyms are sometimes made by adding a prefix.

For example: edible ⟶ inedible

Choose from the prefixes **un**, **in** and **dis** to make each word mean the opposite. Write the antonym in the space provided.

Word	Antonym
safe	unsafe
expensive	inexpensive
willing	unwilling
agree	disagree
complete	incomplete
comfort	discomfort

Complete these sentences using the correct antonym.
Hint: look at the words in italics and use the prefixes you have just learned.

The instructor was clearly not *qualified* to teach the class; therefore, he was unqualified .

At first the magician's assistant was *visible* and then after he said the magic words she was invisible !

I *like* to munch on apples, but I have a strong dislike for apple pie.

p126

Punctuation: getting it right!

There are lots of different types of punctuation, but it is very important to use the correct punctuation in the correct places. Otherwise, the meaning of a sentence may not be clear and will confuse the reader.

Eloise sometimes forgets to use the correct punctuation in her writing. Read her sentences and add the corrections where necessary. Use the key below to add missing punctuation marks. Where a small letter needs to be capital, add a star (*) next to it.

" "	inverted commas/speech marks
.	full stop
,	comma

"I want to go to the beach!" shouted Chloe.

"*is that a clown?" asked Freya.

*it was time to go. It had been a hard day.

"I think that is hilarious," laughed Leon.

"That really hurt!" yelled *leah.

*it has all been worth it.

*daniel bought oranges, apples, bread and milk.

I am going on holiday soon.

Now write a sentence demonstrating the use of each type of punctuation.

Answers may vary

p127

Advanced punctuation

Properly punctuated written English ensures that sentences can be understood clearly and avoids ambiguity, or double meaning.

Match each of the punctuation marks first to its name and then to its definition.

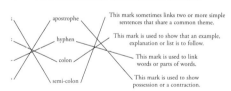

Now read the sentences below carefully and fill in the correct punctuation marks.
Hint: you can also use other punctuation marks that you have already learned.

There's a reason why I didn't go to Adam's party: I didn't have a fancy-dress costume.

Is this café self-service?

It's a really exciting day today; you can tell it's her birthday.

"Is this book yours?" the teacher asked.
"No, it's Zoe's," I replied.

Isobel had an X-ray of her arm.

Don't do that!

p128

Colons and semi-colons in lists

FACTS

Punctuation can be quite complicated and confusing. It is helpful to read written work aloud to help you decide where the punctuation marks should go.

A **colon** (:) is used before a list of words, phrases or clauses. Here is an example. The following were in the boot of the car: beach balls, buckets and spades.

A **semi-colon** (;) is used in a list to separate items that are longer than one or two words. Here is an example. There were several new features in the garden: a pond; a sensory trail along the path; a willow dome; and a bench area for picnics. **Note:** unlike commas, a semi-colon is used before the final item in the list.

Look at the items in the boot of the car below. Write a sentence using a colon to punctuate the list of the items you see.

In the boot of the car were the following: hammer, saw, tool box and boots.

Read the sentence below. It lists a number of items you might find in a garden. Add semi-colons in the right places to separate the items in the list. **Remember:** semi-colons are used to separate items that are longer than one or two words.

These are the items in my shed: a spade to dig the soil;
a watering can to water the plants; a pair of gloves; and
a set of ceramic flower pots.

p129

Colons and semi-colons in lists

FACTS

Colons and semi-colons are also used in bulleted lists. A colon is used before the list begins and semi-colons are used to separate the various items. A full stop is used at the end of the list because it is also the end of the sentence.
Here is an example.

Equipment required for PE:
• shorts;
• T-shirt;
• trainers.

Think of all the things you might need to pack if you were going away on holiday. Then make a list of the items using a colon and semi-colons.

Answers may vary

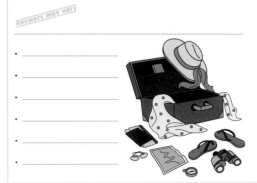

• ....

• ....

• ....

• ....

• ....

• ....

Next time you need to make a list, punctuate it with colons and semi-colons.
It will look pretty impressive!

See if you can spot the use of colons and semi-colons in newspapers and magazines.

p130

Ellipses

FACTS

An **ellipsis** (…) is often used by a writer when he or she wants the reader to fill in the details. Ellipses can also indicate an unfinished thought, a pause or a nervous or awkward silence in writing. For example: **I knew I'd seen his face before…**
Using an ellipsis is a good way of building suspense or mystery in your writing.

Complete each of these sentences by adding words and then ending with an ellipsis.

The three friends .... *Answers may vary*

The door ....

The castle ....

Behind them ....

Through the forest ....

It was a bone-chilling evening ....

Finish writing this opening paragraph of a story. **Note:** use at least one ellipsis to add an element of suspense or mystery.

Daniel and Leah walked slowly towards
the trees. They were excited to have moved
house and be living so close to such
a huge forest.

 *Answers may vary*

p131

Parenthesis: using brackets

BRACKETS

Parenthesis is the use of brackets in a sentence to give more information, explain a difficult word, show thoughts or emphasise a point. For example: the girls **(who were very excited)** couldn't wait to get to the zoo. **Parenthesis** (plural: **parentheses**) is also another word for **bracket**.

Remove the parentheses from these sentences and rearrange them to create two separate sentences.

Merlin and Doodles (our much-loved pet cats) were fighting when Zoe arrived home.
Merlin and Doodles were fighting when Zoe arrived home.
They are our much-loved pet cats.

The headphones (red and black) were very expensive.
The headphones were very expensive.
They are red and black.

The boots (made of black leather) were scuffed and dirty.
The boots were scuffed and dirty.
They are made of black leather.

For each of these pairs of sentences, rewrite them as one sentence that uses parenthesis.

The graph shows the popularity of each football team. The graph is on the previous page.
The graph (on the previous page) shows the popularity
of each football team.

The Eiffel Tower is one of the most iconic landmarks in the world. The Eiffel Tower is found in Paris.
The Eiffel Tower (found in Paris) is one of the most iconic landmarks in the world.

240

Bullet points

Bullet points are used to highlight important information within a piece of text, so that a reader can identify the key points and extract information quickly.

Guidelines for using bullet points:

• The text introducing the bullet points should end with a colon;

• If the text that follows the bullet point is not a complete sentence, it doesn't need to start with a capital letter;

• If the text following the bullet point is a complete sentence, it should begin with a capital letter;

• You can end the text following each bullet point with a semi-colon, no punctuation at all, or a full stop if it is a complete sentence. The text following the last bullet point, however, should always end with a full stop.

Here is a picture of Flib-Flob the Alien. Write bullet points to describe him. The first one has been done for you.

This alien:

• has large oval eyes; *Answers may vary*

• ....

• ....

• ....

Use bullet points to make a list of the main points of a book you have recently read.

The main points are:

• ....

• ....

• .... *Answers may vary*

• ....

See if you can find examples of bullet points in newspapers and magazines.

Apostrophe to show possession

As well as being used in contractions (such as **we'll** and **shouldn't**), apostrophes are used to show possession, or ownership, as in **the peacock's feathers** or in **one month's time**. Apostrophes showing possession can go in two places, depending on the number of possessors. For one possessor, the apostrophe is placed before an added s, as in **the cat's food**. This refers to food belonging to one cat. For more than one possessor, the apostrophe is placed at the end of the plural word, as in **the cats' food**. This refers to food belonging to more than one cat.

There are exceptions to these rules. For example: singular words that end in s can end with just an apostrophe (') or an apostrophe and s ('s).
For example: **Charles' birthday** and **Charles's birthday** are both acceptable.

Draw a line to match each phrase with apostrophes to the number of brothers and friends it refers to. Think carefully before you start.

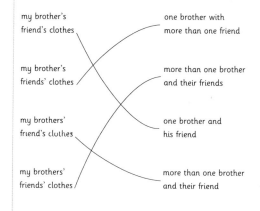

my brother's friend's clothes — one brother and his friend

my brother's friends' clothes — one brother with more than one friend

my brothers' friend's clothes — more than one brother and their friend

my brothers' friends' clothes — more than one brother and their friends

Homophones

A **homophone** is a word that is pronounced, or sounds, the same as another word but has a different spelling and meaning. For example: **sun** and **son**.

Read the passage below and underline the homophones that you think have been spelled incorrectly. Then make a list of the correct spellings in the space under the passage.

It was late one wintry Sunday <u>knight</u>. A young elf, with an outrageously long beard and matted <u>hare</u>, was sitting on a toadstool eating magic <u>serial</u>. His friends thought it strange that he liked to eat <u>serial</u> at <u>knight</u>, but even stranger were the contents of the <u>serial</u>! The bowl, <u>witch</u> was full to the brim, contained <u>currents</u>, a <u>peace</u> of <u>would</u>, the herb <u>time</u> and the stumpy <u>tale</u> of a wild <u>bare</u>! The elf didn't really care <u>weather</u> his friends thought it strange. He simply ignored them when they <u>wood</u> pass and <u>stair</u>.

night	piece	
hair	wood	
cereal	thyme	whether
which	tail	would
currants	bear	stare

Words with "ie" and "ei"

The spelling rhyme "I before E, except after C" is well known, but it does not always apply.

The rule does apply:

• when the letters together make a long **e** sound, as in **deceit** and **shield**.

The rule does not apply:

• when the letters together make a long **a** sound, as in **sleigh**;

• when using the plural form for words ending in **cy**, as in **pregnancies**;

• when the letters **i** and **e** are pronounced as separate vowels in words, as in **science**.

Write the missing **ie** or **ei** in the space provided below. **Remember:** think carefully about the rule and its exceptions before completing the words.

c**ei**ling	polic**ie**s	shr**ie**k
f**ie**ld	pric**ie**r	soc**ie**ty
fr**ei**ght	rec**ei**pt	th**ie**f
frequenc**ie**s	rec**ei**ve	vacanc**ie**s
n**ei**ghbour	r**ei**gn	v**ei**l
p**ie**ce	rel**ie**f	w**ei**ght

Can you think of any exceptions? Here are some clues:

A part of our diet	protein
Eerie or strange	weird
To grab hold	seize

Direct speech

You use **direct speech** to write down exactly what a person says. You must enclose the words being said within inverted commas.
For example: **"I have no idea what is going on!" said Mrs Wilson.**

Write down what the aliens Bee-Bee and Bo-Bo are saying in the speech bubbles as direct speech. Make sure you put inverted commas around their words, followed by **asked Bo-Bo** or **replied Bee-Bee**.
Remember: start a new line each time a new person, or character, speaks.

Bee-Bee, what time will the space shuttle arrive?

Bo-Bo, I think it will be eight o'clock.

"Bee-Bee, what time will the space
shuttle arrive?" asked Bo-Bo.
"Bo-Bo, I think it will be eight o'clock," replied Bee-Bee.

What shall we do tonight?

Have a party!

"What shall we do tonight?" asked Bo-Bo.
"Have a party!" replied Bee-Bee.

Are you looking forward to seeing all our friends?

Not really. I like it here with just us two.

"Are you looking forward to seeing all
our friends?" asked Bo-Bo.
"Not really. I like it here with just us two," replied Bee-Bee.

Reported speech

You use **reported speech** to write what has been said, but you do not use the exact spoken words. You report it in your own words as the writer.
For example: **Mrs White said that she was so pleased with her class.**

Imagine you are writing a report about the new aliens landing on the planet where Bo-Bo and Bee-Bee live. Using reported speech, write next to the aliens what they said about the new visitors.

Answers may vary

I could not believe my eyes!

Bo-Bo said he could not believe what he saw.

Bee-Bee was worried that the new aliens might
take over his planet.

Will the new aliens take over our planet?

I think they will be friendly, like us.

Bo-Bo thought they would be friendly
aliens, just like himself and Bee-Bee.

Now try writing a report of an event you have been involved in, such as a birthday celebration or a sporting event at school.

Formal and informal speech

Formal speech is used in official writing and situations, such as legal documents, news reports, business letters and official speeches. **Informal speech** is used in everyday conversations and personal letters or emails.

Read the three different letters numbered 1, 2 and 3. Then, write the corresponding numbers in the three small boxes at the bottom of the page, in order from most formal to least formal (informal).

1
Dear Kayte,

I have been to the beach today and the weather was great. I went swimming! I hope to see you soon,

Lots of love,
Claire

2
To Whom it May Concern,

Today I went to a beautiful beach on the south coast. We were lucky that the weather was really good for this time of year. We also had the opportunity to go swimming, which meant we all got some well-needed exercise. I look forward to hearing from you.

Kind regards,
Ms C White

3
Hi Kayte!

Been to beach. Great weather. Went swimming.

See you soon.
Claire

Most formal   Least formal

2 → 1 → 3

Formal and informal speech

Formal and informal writing and speech differ from each other in tone and structure.

Write a letter to your friend telling him or her about your last holiday.
Think about whether you will write the letter in formal or informal speech.

Answers may vary

Points of view

A story or any other type of writing can be written from different points of view. If it is written from the writer's point of view, it is said to be in the first person. For example: **I saw a spaceship in the sky.**
When the point of view is that of an outside observer, it is said to be in the third person. For example: **Sophie saw a spaceship in the sky.**

Read each sentence below carefully. Write **first person** or **third person** next to each, depending on the point of view.

Every summer, I look forward to the warm evenings. _____first person_____

The hedgehog curled up inside the hollow log.
He got himself ready for the long, sleepy winter. _____third person_____

When I heard the birds chirping, I knew it was the break
of dawn. _____first person_____

I feel proud of everything my daughter has achieved. _____first person_____

Katy knew how well she had done at Irish dancing and
was full of pride. _____third person_____

The hairdresser asked Alena, "Just the usual cut today?"
Alena wondered if she should try something new. _____third person_____

I am going on holiday soon. _____first person_____

Write two sentences: one in the first person and another in the third person.

....

....

Personification

Personification is a figure of speech in which non-human things are described as having human characteristics, as in **the blushing sun** or **the angry storm**. This type of **figurative language** is often used in poetry. It can help create a vivid picture in the mind of the reader.

Read this poem. Extract the lines using personification and rewrite them below.

It's Coming!
I can smell it in the air; I can feel it in my bones,
It's coming!
Light creeps away,
Dark is dawning on us,
Raindrops frown as they start to pummel the colourless pavement,
It's coming!
Whispering trees dance in the howling wind,
It's grey gravel gravitating downwards from the stormy skies above,
It's coming!
Hail starts to break through the thick murky cotton wool,
Cold crystal tears streaming down pale cheek,
It's coming!
Streaks of light strike the innocent houses below.
The tempest is here.

Alisha Charlton (age 11)

Raindrops frown as they start to pummel the colourless pavement

Whispering trees dance in the howling wind

Cold crystal tears streaming down pale cheek

Now match each season to its personification below.

Spring ——————— His icy cold fingers cling to the branches.

Summer ——————— His light steps bring new life to everything he touches.

Autumn ——————— Her skin is dry and wrinkled, lifeless and bare.

Winter ——————— Her hair is a blaze of light, shedding warmth to those around her.

Exploring synonyms

Synonyms are words with the same or similar meaning, such as **happy** and **content** or **ill** and **poorly**. Words that are synonyms of each other are said to be synonymous.

Draw a line to match each pair of synonyms below.

buy ——————— large
big ——————— on
quickly ——————— purchase
upon ——————— speedily

Write each of the words from the exercise above under one of these headings.

Verb	Adjective	Adverb	Preposition
buy	big	quickly	on
purchase	large	speedily	upon

Now think of a synonym to go with each of the adjectives below.

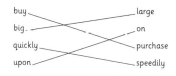

dangerous .... risky

small .... tiny

clever .... intelligent

broad .... wide

wealthy .... rich

slender .... slim

Synonyms for "said"

Synonyms help improve your writing and make it more engaging. For instance, using synonyms of the word **said**, which is often overused, will make your writing more interesting. When doing this, think carefully about how the character is speaking and what is being said.

The characters below are saying something in a certain way. Think of a synonym for **said** that reflects the way they are speaking. Then, write the sentence using the synonym. The first one has been done for you.

What is said	How it is said	Synonym and sentence
"I am going to the Wizardland."	in a happy way	beamed "I am going to the Wizardland!" beamed the girl.
"They said I couldn't climb the magic tree."	in a sad way	moaned "They said I couldn't climb the magic tree," moaned the pixie.
"It's not my fault!"	in a frightened way	stuttered "It's not my fault!" stuttered the mouse.
"This way, my lady."	as an answer	replied "This way, my lady," replied the prince.

Types of sentence

A **simple sentence** has one subject and one verb. For example: **Phoebe lives in France.**

A **compound sentence** has two main clauses, which could both stand on their own as separate sentences, joined by a connective. For example: **Phoebe lives in France, but I live in England.**

A **complex sentence** has a main clause and one or more subordinate clauses, joined by a connective. A subordinate clause contains a subject and a verb, but it needs to be attached to a main clause because it does not make much sense on its own. For example: **I first met Phoebe in Paris, where I lived as a small child.**

Study the picture below. Then write a simple, a compound and a complex sentence based on this picture.

Answers may vary

Simple sentence

....

....

Compound sentence

....

....

Complex sentence

....

....

Clauses and connectives

When a sentence has two clauses, a connective is used to join them together. The clauses may be two main clauses, making a compound sentence, or a main clause and a subordinate clause, making a complex sentence. Common connectives include **and**, **which**, **although**, **after**, **before** and **so**.

Read the sentences below. Draw one line under the main clause, two lines under the subordinate clause and a circle around the connective. Reread the opposite page to help you. The first one has been done for you.

I like apples (and) I like oranges.

I could go the beach (or) I could stay home.

Zoe wanted some new clothes, (so) she went shopping.

Peter took three biscuits, (which) he later gave to Isobel.

Before Zoe went to school, Isobel came round for breakfast.

Amy watched TV (after) she had finished her homework.

I tried to explain to Anna, (although) she didn't understand.

Active and passive

Active sentences describe an action done **by the subject.**
   I directed the award-winning film. (an **active** sentence)
Passive sentences describe an action done **to the subject.**
   The award-winning film was directed by me. (a **passive** sentence)

Change these sentences from **passive** to **active**.

The match was won by our team.
Our team won the match.

The winning goal was scored by Rachel.
Rachel scored the winning goal.

The party was enjoyed by all my friends.
All my friends enjoyed the party.

Jack was stung by an unusual insect.
An unusual insect stung Jack.

Now change these sentences from **active** to **passive**.

Aliens invade our planet.
Our planet is invaded by aliens.

Leonardo da Vinci painted the *Mona Lisa.*
The Mona Lisa was painted by Leonardo da Vinci.

The team dislike the group leader.
The group leader is disliked by the team.

The hero piloted his craft with great skill.
The hero's craft was piloted with great skill.

A hurricane struck the town.
The town was struck by a hurricane.

Paragraphs and punctuation

Rewrite the following passage in **paragraphs**, **punctuating** it and changing small letters into capital letters where necessary.
Remember: Paragraphs separate ideas, themes or instructions. Without paragraphs, writing can be difficult to understand.

rainbows
my heart leaps up when i behold a rainbow in the sky wrote william wordsworth the famous poet and most of us share his feelings when we are lucky enough to see a rainbow there is an old saying that a pot of gold is buried at the end of the rainbow but have you ever tried to reach a rainbows end of course its impossible because a rainbow is really just the result of the raindrops refracting and reflecting light from our sun there are seven colours in the rainbow red orange yellow green blue indigo and violet

"My heart leaps up when I behold a rainbow in the sky," wrote William Wordsworth, the famous English poet, and most of us share his feelings when we are lucky enough to see a rainbow.

There is an old saying that a pot of gold is buried at the end of the rainbow, but have you ever tried to reach a rainbow's end? Of course it's impossible, because a rainbow is really just the result of the raindrops refracting and reflecting light from our Sun.

There are seven colours in the rainbow: red, orange, , yellow, green, blue, indigo and violet.

Rewrite this section of a **play script** as a **story**. Use **paragraphs** and **speech marks**. Write on a separate sheet of paper, and continue the story, if you wish.
Remember: When writing **direct speech** (dialogue), start a new paragraph each time the speaker changes.

"It's raining again, but the sun is shining as well," said Nick.
"I think we should go swimming anyway," said Sophie.
"We might get wet … let's wait a bit longer," suggested Nick.
"We can't swim without getting wet, Nick. What difference does it make?" Sophie asked.
"Hey!" exclaimed Nick.
"What is it?" asked Sophie.
"Look – a rainbow over the beach!" cried Nick.
"Quick, get your spade – we'll be rich!" exclaimed Sophie.

p155 **1)** 10 **2)** –5 **3)** –2 **4)** 5

p157 **1)** 170cm **2)** 200cm

p161 **multiples of 8:** 16, 32, 48, 56, 64, 72, 144
multiples of 9: 18, 27, 36, 72, 81, 90, 108, 144
common multiples: 72, 144

p169 **1)** ¹⁄₁₂ **2)** ¹⁄₁₀ **3)** ¹⁄₂₁ **4)** ⅙

p171 Twerg 17.24, Bloop 16.56, Glook 17.21, Kwonk 16.13, Zarg 16.01. Zarg's time is fastest.

p172 **1)** 75% **2)** 50% **3)** 40%

p173 **1)** 20 **2)** 55 **3)** 80

p177 **1)** 37 **2)** 17 **3)** 65

p178 The other nets of a cube are:

p181 **1)** 30° **2)** 120°

p183 115°

p185 **1)** (2, 0), (1, 3), (–3, 3), (–4, 0), (–3, –3), (1, –3).
2) You would make this shape:

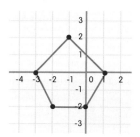

p187 **1)** 133 **2)** 7 **3)** 19

p191 **1)** 155° **2)** 20%

p193 **1)** 32 **2)** 7 **3)** 53 **4)** 21

p195 **1)** 44, 50, 56, 62, 68 **2)** (6 x 40)+ 2 = 242 **3)** (6 x 100) + 2 = 602

---

p200

Factors, multiples, and prime numbers

Write all the factors of these numbers.

12	1, 2, 3, 4, 6, 12
25	1, 5, 25
72	1, 2, 3, 4, 6, 8, 9, 12, 18, 24, 36, 72
18	1, 2, 3, 6, 9, 18
64	1, 2, 4, 8, 16, 32, 64
96	1, 2, 3, 4, 6, 8, 12, 16, 24, 32, 48, 96

What are the common factors of these numbers?

15 and 25	1, 5
72 and 108	1, 2, 3, 4, 6, 9, 12, 18, 36
48 and 64	1, 2, 4, 8, 16
150 and 125	1, 5, 25

Circle the multiples of these numbers.

Multiples of 3	⑨	⑮	26	㉝	62
Multiples of 5	17	㉕	43	⑦⓪	㊾
Multiples of 8	26	㉜	㊶	62	㊉

Write the first three common multiples of these numbers.

3 and 5	15, 30, 45
4 and 7	28, 56, 84

Write the prime numbers between these numbers.

1 and 20	2, 3, 5, 7, 11, 13, 17, 19
20 and 50	23, 29, 31, 37, 41, 43, 47

---

p201

Add and subtract fractions

Work out these calculations.

$$\frac{1}{4} + \frac{5}{6} = \frac{3}{12} + \frac{10}{12} = \frac{13}{12} = 1\frac{1}{12}$$

$$\frac{7}{9} - \frac{2}{3} = \frac{7}{9} - \frac{6}{9} = \frac{1}{9}$$

Remember: Use equivalent fractions to make the denominators the same.

Add these fractions. Give answers as improper fractions if necessary.

$$\frac{1}{3} + \frac{1}{3} = \frac{2}{3} \qquad \frac{4}{11} + \frac{3}{4} = \frac{49}{44} \qquad \frac{6}{9} + \frac{12}{18} = \frac{24}{18} \qquad \frac{3}{5} + \frac{4}{10} = \frac{10}{10}$$

$$\frac{3}{8} + \frac{2}{8} = \frac{5}{8} \qquad \frac{1}{5} + \frac{3}{5} = \frac{4}{5} \qquad \frac{2}{5} + \frac{6}{15} = \frac{12}{15} \qquad \frac{4}{7} + \frac{2}{5} = \frac{34}{35}$$

$$\frac{2}{6} + \frac{3}{12} = \frac{7}{12} \qquad \frac{5}{9} + \frac{3}{9} = \frac{8}{9} \qquad \frac{2}{7} + \frac{4}{7} = \frac{6}{7} \qquad \frac{2}{5} + \frac{3}{9} = \frac{33}{45}$$

$$\frac{5}{8} + \frac{4}{12} = \frac{23}{24} \qquad \frac{1}{4} + \frac{3}{8} = \frac{5}{8} \qquad \frac{4}{10} + \frac{3}{10} = \frac{7}{10}$$

Add these mixed fractions. Give answers as mixed fractions.
Remember: First change them to improper fractions.

$$1\frac{1}{4} + 3\frac{1}{4} = 4\frac{1}{2} \qquad 3\frac{1}{3} + 4\frac{1}{2} = 7\frac{5}{6} \qquad 2\frac{2}{5} + 2\frac{3}{5} = 5$$

$$2\frac{3}{4} + 1\frac{2}{3} = 4\frac{5}{12} \qquad 1\frac{4}{5} + 3\frac{3}{10} = 5\frac{1}{10} \qquad 4\frac{5}{8} + 2\frac{3}{4} = 7\frac{3}{8}$$

Subtract these fractions. Write answers in simplest form.

$$\frac{3}{5} - \frac{2}{5} = \frac{1}{5} \qquad \frac{3}{4} - \frac{7}{12} = \frac{1}{6} \qquad \frac{3}{5} - \frac{1}{3} = \frac{4}{15} \qquad \frac{1}{3} - \frac{1}{4} = \frac{1}{12}$$

$$\frac{4}{5} - \frac{7}{10} = \frac{1}{10} \qquad \frac{5}{8} - \frac{3}{8} = \frac{1}{4} \qquad \frac{11}{15} - \frac{2}{5} = \frac{1}{3} \qquad \frac{1}{2} - \frac{2}{7} = \frac{3}{14}$$

$$\frac{2}{3} - \frac{4}{9} = \frac{2}{9} \qquad \frac{5}{6} - \frac{2}{3} = \frac{1}{6} \qquad \frac{7}{9} - \frac{2}{9} = \frac{5}{9} \qquad \frac{1}{2} - \frac{5}{12} = \frac{1}{12}$$

Subtract these mixed fractions. Give answers in simplest form.
Remember: First change them to improper fractions.

$$4\frac{2}{5} - 3\frac{4}{5} = \frac{3}{5} \qquad 2\frac{5}{8} - 1\frac{7}{8} = \frac{3}{4} \qquad 5\frac{4}{9} - 4\frac{2}{9} = 1\frac{2}{9}$$

$$2\frac{2}{3} - 1\frac{3}{4} = \frac{11}{12} \qquad 2\frac{1}{2} - 2\frac{3}{8} = \frac{1}{8} \qquad 4\frac{5}{6} - 3\frac{2}{3} = 1\frac{1}{6}$$

p202 — Multiply fractions

p202

Work out these calculations.

$$\frac{2}{3} \times \frac{1}{2} = \frac{2 \times 1}{3 \times 2} = \frac{2}{6} = \frac{1}{3}$$
$$\frac{2}{5} \times 2 = \frac{2}{5} \times \frac{2}{1} = \frac{2 \times 2}{5 \times 1} = \frac{4}{5}$$

Multiply these fractions. Give answers in their simplest form.

$\frac{3}{4} \times \frac{1}{2} = \frac{3}{8}$ $\frac{3}{5} \times \frac{2}{3} = \frac{2}{5}$

$\frac{3}{10} \times \frac{2}{5} = \frac{3}{25}$ $\frac{1}{2} \times \frac{3}{7} = \frac{3}{14}$

$\frac{2}{3} \times \frac{1}{4} = \frac{1}{6}$ $\frac{5}{8} \times \frac{2}{4} = \frac{5}{16}$

$\frac{7}{10} \times \frac{3}{4} = \frac{21}{40}$ $\frac{1}{2} \times \frac{5}{8} = \frac{5}{16}$

$\frac{2}{3} \times \frac{4}{10} = \frac{4}{15}$ $\frac{3}{5} \times \frac{2}{6} = \frac{1}{5}$

$\frac{4}{9} \times \frac{1}{3} = \frac{4}{27}$ $\frac{2}{3} \times \frac{5}{6} = \frac{5}{9}$

Multiply these fractions by whole numbers. Give answers as mixed fractions.

$\frac{2}{3} \times 4 = 2\frac{2}{3}$ $\frac{3}{5} \times 2 = 1\frac{1}{5}$

$\frac{3}{4} \times 6 = 4\frac{1}{2}$ $\frac{3}{10} \times 5 = 1\frac{1}{2}$

$\frac{5}{8} \times 3 = 1\frac{7}{8}$ $\frac{4}{7} \times 8 = 4\frac{4}{7}$

$\frac{1}{5} \times 9 = 1\frac{4}{5}$ $\frac{1}{4} \times 4 = 1$

$\frac{5}{12} \times 3 = 1\frac{1}{4}$ $\frac{6}{11} \times 2 = 1\frac{1}{11}$

$\frac{5}{9} \times 3 = 1\frac{2}{3}$ $\frac{10}{100} \times 4 = \frac{2}{5}$

p203 — Divide fractions

p203

Work out these calculations.

$$\frac{1}{3} \div 2 = \frac{1}{3} \div \frac{2}{1} = \frac{1}{3} \times \frac{1}{2} = \frac{1}{6}$$
$$\frac{4}{7} \div \frac{3}{5} = \frac{4}{7} \times \frac{5}{3} = \frac{4 \times 5}{7 \times 3} = \frac{20}{21}$$

Divide these fractions by whole numbers. Give answers in their simplest form.

$\frac{1}{3} \div 3 = \frac{1}{9}$ $\frac{4}{5} \div 2 = \frac{2}{5}$

$\frac{3}{8} \div 2 = \frac{3}{16}$ $\frac{1}{4} \div 6 = \frac{1}{24}$

$\frac{1}{2} \div 5 = \frac{1}{10}$ $\frac{3}{4} \div 7 = \frac{3}{28}$

$\frac{7}{10} \div 3 = \frac{7}{30}$ $\frac{2}{9} \div 5 = \frac{2}{45}$

$\frac{3}{7} \div 3 = \frac{1}{7}$ $\frac{2}{5} \div 4 = \frac{1}{10}$

$\frac{2}{3} \div 6 = \frac{1}{9}$ $\frac{5}{6} \div 3 = \frac{5}{18}$

Divide these fractions. Give answers as a mixed number if needed.

$\frac{1}{2} \div \frac{1}{3} = 1\frac{1}{2}$ $\frac{3}{4} \div \frac{2}{3} = 1\frac{1}{8}$

$\frac{3}{5} \div \frac{1}{6} = 3\frac{3}{5}$ $\frac{5}{7} \div \frac{2}{5} = 1\frac{11}{14}$

$\frac{2}{9} \div \frac{3}{5} = \frac{10}{27}$ $\frac{5}{8} \div \frac{1}{2} = 1\frac{1}{4}$

$\frac{7}{10} \div \frac{1}{4} = 2\frac{4}{5}$ $\frac{3}{7} \div \frac{4}{9} = \frac{27}{28}$

$\frac{4}{5} \div \frac{5}{6} = \frac{24}{25}$ $\frac{1}{4} \div \frac{3}{10} = \frac{5}{6}$

$\frac{2}{5} \div \frac{1}{3} = 1\frac{1}{5}$ $\frac{1}{8} \div \frac{9}{10} = \frac{5}{36}$

p204 — Ratio and proportion

p204

A rat has 7 babies every 4 months.
How many babies does the rat have in one year?   21

In a class, there are 2 girls for every 3 boys.
There are 10 girls. How many boys are there?   15 boys

In a week, a dog eats 4 cans of dog food with 7 biscuits.
How many biscuits are needed for 24 cans?   42 biscuits

A cook uses 6 apples with 300 g flour to make an apple crumble. How many apples are needed with 1.5 kg of flour?   30 apples

In a bathroom, a black tile is used for every 5 white tiles. How many black tiles are needed for 60 white tiles?   12 black tiles

An account earns £2.50 interest for every £10 000 saved. How much interest is earned on £150 000?   £37.50

A rectangle is drawn with length 5 cm x width 8 cm. If it is drawn 4 times larger with length 20 cm, what is the width?   32 cm

A model of a building uses the scale 10 cm = 200 ft. The model of the building is 75 cm high. What is the actual height going to be?   1500 ft

p205 — Algebra

p205

Work out this equation.

$a + 5 = 7$
$a + 5\,(-5) = 7\,(-5)$
$a = 2$

$10 - b = 4$
$10 - b\,(+b) = 4\,(+b)$
$10\,(-4) = 4 + b\,(-4)$
$b = 6$

$a + 4 = 14 - 6$
$a + 4 = 8$
$a + 4\,(-4) = 8\,(-4)$
$a = 4$

Find value of each letter.

$a + 6 = 24$ $a = 18$ $b - 5 = 14$ $b = 19$

$a + 28 = 42$ $a = 14$ $b - 17 = 17$ $b = 34$

$a + 17 = 25$ $a = 8$ $b - 27 = 23$ $b = 50$

$10 + y = 12$ $y = 2$ $16 - x = 4$ $x = 12$

$38 + y = 50$ $y = 12$ $26 - x = 9$ $x = 17$

$42 + y = 64$ $y = 22$ $42 - x = 20$ $x = 22$

Solve these equations.

$15 + a = 42 - 17$ $a = 10$ $y + 13 = 7 \times 5$ $y = 22$

$100 - b = 72 + 14$ $b = 14$ $x - 42 = 96 \div 8$ $x = 54$

$63 + a = 9 \times 9$ $a = 18$ $21 - y = 40 - 25$ $y = 6$

Write equations for these problems and then solve them.

Laura had a bookcase overloaded with books. She gave 24 to a school fair. She had 36 left. How many books did she have to begin with? $b - 24 = 36$ so $b = 60$

Dan collected comics. He was given a set of 12 for his birthday. He now had 64 in his collection. How many comics did he have before his birthday? $c + 12 = 64$ so $c = 52$

p206 — Decimal addition

Write the answer to each sum.

296.48 + 131.74 428.22	173.05 + 269.23 442.28

Write the answer to each sum.

491.83 + 137.84 629.67	964.71 + 321.26 1285.97	302.04 + 204.99 507.03	306.25 + 844.24 1150.49
471.93 + 755.26 1227.19	842.01 + 711.84 1553.85	675.82 + 105.23 781.05	137.82 + 399.71 537.53
465.24 + 605.27 1070.51	178.93 + 599.41 778.34	184.74 + 372.81 557.55	443.27 + 705.99 1149.26
563.23 + 413.98 977.21	703.95 + 685.11 1389.06	825.36 + 249.85 1075.21	529.33 + 482.56 1011.89

Write the answer to each sum.

421.79 + 136.25 =   558.04   192.31 + 241.73 =   434.04

558.32 + 137.94 =   696.26   501.84 + 361.93 =   863.77

227.66 + 142.07 =   369.73   275.31 + 239.33 =   514.64

153.31 + 189.02 =   342.33   491.44 + 105.37 =   596.81

253.71 + 562.41 =   816.12   829.25 + 163.74 =   992.99

p207 — Problems with negative numbers

What is the difference in temperature between Boston and Barcelona?

11°C

By how much would the temperature have to go up in Boston to be the same as London?

9°C

City	Temperature
Boston	–9°C
Barcelona	2°C
London	0°C

City	Temperature
Athens	2°C
New York	–6°C
Tokyo	1°C

City	Temperature
Warsaw	–7°C
Zurich	–12°C
Rome	5°C

By how much is Athens warmer than Warsaw?   9°C

If the temperature went up by 5°C, what would it be in:

New York   –1°C   Zurich   –7°C   Warsaw   –2°C

If the temperature went down by 6°C, what would it be in:

Tokyo   –5°C   Rome   –1°C   Athens   –4°C

The temperature outside is –11°C. If it rises by 7°C, what is the new temperature?   –4°C

The temperature inside a shelter is 5°C. The temperature outside is 12°C lower. What is the temperature outside?   –7°C

The frozen food compartments in a supermarket are kept at a constant temperature of –7°C. During a power cut the temperature rises to 10°C. By how much has the temperature risen?   17°C

The temperature at midnight is –8°C. At midday it is 15°C higher. What is the temperature at midday?   7°C

p208 — Real life problems

A man walks 18.34 km on Saturday and 16.57 km on Sunday. How far did he walk that weekend?

34.91 km

18.34 + 16.57 34.91

How much further did he walk on Saturday?

1.77 km

18.34 – 16.57 1.77

A rectangular field measures 103.7 m by 96.5 m. How long is the perimeter of the field?

400.4 m

103.7 × 2 207.4	207.4 +193.0 400.4
	96.5 × 2 193.0

When Joe and Kerry stand on a weighing machine it reads 136.53 kg. When Joe steps off, it reads 68.76 kg. How much does Joe weigh?

67.77kg

136.53 – 68.76 67.77

A rectangular room has an area of 32.58 m². When a carpet is put down there is still 7.99 m² of floor showing. How large is the area of the carpet?

24.59 m²

32.58 – 7.99 24.59

A brother and sister's combined height is 3.27 m. If the sister is 1.59 m tall, how tall is the brother?

1.68 m

3.27 – 1.59 1.68

A country has 4 motorways, the MA which is 1 246 km long, the MB which is 339 km long, the MC which is 1 573 km long, and the MD which is 48 km long. How much motorway does the country have in total?

3 206 Km

1246 339 1573 + 48 3206

Jenny's aquarium holds 25.56 litres of water. She buys a new one which holds 32 litres. How much extra water do her fish have?

6.44 litres

32.00 – 25.56 6.44

p209 — Simple use of brackets

Work out these calculations.

(4 + 6) – (2 + 1) =   10 – 3 = 7

(2 x 5) + (10 – 4) =   10 + 6 = 16

Work out the brackets first.

Work out these calculations.

(5 + 3) + (6 – 2) =   12   (3 – 1) + (12 – 1) =   13

(6 – 1) – (1 + 2) =   2   (9 + 5) – (3 + 6) =   5

(8 + 3) + (12 – 2) =   21   (14 + 12) – (9 + 4) =   13

(7 – 2) + (4 + 5)=   14   (9 – 3) – (4 + 2) =   0

Now try these longer calculations.

(5 + 9)   +   (12 – 2) – (4 + 3) =   17

(10 + 5)   –   (2 + 4) + (9 + 6) =   24

(19 + 4)   –   (3 + 2) – (2 + 1) =   15

(24 – 5)   –   (3 + 7) – (5 – 2) =   6

(15 + 3)   +   (7 – 2) – (5 + 7) =   11

Now try these. Be careful, the brackets now have multiplication calculations.

(2 x 3) + (5 x 2) =   16   (3 x 4) – (2 x 2) =   8

(7 x 2) + (3 x 3) =   23   (5 x 4) – (3 x 2) =   14

(6 x 4) – (4 x 3) =   12   (9 x 5) – (4 x 6) =   21

(12 x 4) – (8 x 3) =   24   (7 x 4) – (8 x 2) =   12

If the answer is 24, which of these calculations gives the correct answer? Write the letter in the box.

a (3 + 5)+ (3 x 1)   c (3 x 5) + (3 x 3)   e (5 x 7) – (2 x 5)
b (3 x 5) + (3 x 2)   d (2 x 5) + (2 x 6)   f (6 + 7) + (12 – 2)

(c)

Multiplying decimals

Work out these calculations.

1.456	1.456	1.456	1.456
x 10	x 20	x 3	x 23
14.56	29.12	4.368	29.120
			+ 4.368
			33.488

Multiply these numbers.

2.567	4.687	8.924	3.963
x 10	x 10	x 100	x 100
25.67	46.87	892.4	396.3

12.892	7.689	9.578	15.432
x 100	x 1000	x 1000	x 1000
1289.2	7689	9578	15432

Multiply these numbers.

0.456	0.351	1.764	14.23
x 2	x 4	x 8	x 3
0.912	1.404	14.112	42.69

0.859	1.034	8.049	69.23
x 7	x 6	x 5	x 3
6.013	6.204	40.245	207.69

2.836	0.765	5.218	62.73
x 12	x 18	x 30	x 45
28.360	7.650	156.54	2509.20
+ 5.672	+ 6.120		+ 313.65
34.032	13.770		2822.85

1.873	20.72	708.7	8.302
x 60	x 21	x 15	x 40
112.38	415.40	7087.0	332.08
	+ 20.72	+ 3543.5	
	435.12	10630.5	

Division by units

47÷2 can be written in two ways:

$23\frac{1}{2}$ or 23.5
2⟌47   2⟌47.0

Write the answers to these calculations with fraction remainders (amounts left over).

$8\frac{1}{2}$	$4\frac{3}{4}$	$5\frac{1}{3}$	$9\frac{1}{4}$
2⟌17	4⟌19	3⟌16	4⟌37

$9\frac{2}{3}$	$22\frac{1}{2}$	$17\frac{2}{5}$	$9\frac{4}{5}$
3⟌29	2⟌45	5⟌87	5⟌49

$18\frac{1}{4}$	$11\frac{2}{3}$	$23\frac{1}{4}$	$13\frac{4}{5}$
4⟌73	3⟌35	4⟌93	5⟌69

Write the answers to these calculations with decimal remainders.

36.5	42.5	19.5	14.75
2⟌73	2⟌85	2⟌39	4⟌59

17.75	20.75	5.8	9.4
4⟌71	4⟌83	5⟌29	5⟌47

4.8	38.5	9.5	18.6
5⟌24	2⟌77	4⟌38	5⟌93

Write the answers to these calculations choosing decimal or fraction remainders.

18.5 or $18\frac{1}{2}$	29.5 or $29\frac{1}{2}$	23.25 or $23\frac{1}{4}$	12.75 or $12\frac{3}{4}$
2⟌37	2⟌59	4⟌93	4⟌51

4.2 or $4\frac{1}{5}$	41.5 or $41\frac{1}{2}$	7.75 or $7\frac{3}{4}$	12.6 or $12\frac{3}{5}$
5⟌21	2⟌83	4⟌31	5⟌63

Division of 3-digit decimal numbers

Work out these division calculations.

1.99	1.61
5⟌9.95	6⟌9.66

Work out these division calculations.

1.63	1.85	1.27	1.06
5⟌8.15	5⟌9.25	5⟌6.35	6⟌6.36

0.36	1.26	0.69	0.74
6⟌2.16	7⟌8.82	7⟌4.83	8⟌5.92

1.09	0.91	0.63	1.52
8⟌8.72	9⟌8.19	9⟌5.67	6⟌9.12

0.99	1.06	0.38	1.35
6⟌5.94	8⟌8.48	7⟌2.66	7⟌9.45

0.84	1.18	0.61	1.31
9⟌7.56	8⟌9.44	7⟌4.27	7⟌9.17

Write the answer in the box.

What is 8.82 divided by 9?	0.98	Find $\frac{1}{8}$ of 9.28	1.16
What is 8.22 divided by 6?	1.37	Find $\frac{1}{9}$ of 5.85	0.65
Share 3.78 equally among 6	0.63	What is 3.12 divided by 8?	0.39

Work out the answer to each calculation.

Sammy spends £2.85 a week on his bus fares to school. How much is his bus fare each day?

57 p

A fence is 9.48 metres long. If it is made up of 6 panels, how long is each panel?

1.58 m

Real life problems

A family is driving 120 km to visit friends. If they have already driven 30% of the distance, how far have they travelled?

$\frac{120 \times 30}{100} =$ 36 km

Mr Chang gets a £500 bonus from his firm. He puts 40% in the bank and spends the rest. How much does he put in the bank?

£200

How much does he spend?

£300

$\frac{500 \times 40}{100} = 200$

500 − 200 = 300

A school has 300 children. 55% of them are girls. How many boys are there in the school?

135 boys

$\frac{300 \times 45}{100} = 135$

In a spelling test of 80 words Sinead gets 75% right. How many does she get wrong?

20 words wrong

$\frac{\cancel{80} \times 25}{\cancel{100}} = 20$

A man wins £5 000 on the lottery. If he gives 25% to charity, how much does he keep for himself?

£3 750

$\frac{5000 \times 75}{100} = 3750$

A team of 5 people works from 09:00 until 17:00 every day. If they each have an hour's lunch break, how many hours do they work altogether between Monday and Friday?

175 hours

17:00
− 9:00
8:00   8 − 1 = 7

7 × 5 = 35
35 × 5 = 175

A train leaves at 08:47 and arrives at 16:29. How long does the journey take?

7 hours 42 mins

16:29
− 8:47
7:42

Reading from scales

What does this scale read?

76 g

What do these scales read?

93 g

49 g

6 g

22 g

35 g

1.4 kg

3.7 kg

1.8 kg

Mean, median, and mode

Sian throws a dice 7 times. Here are her results:

4, 2, 1, 2, 4, 2, 6

What is the mean? $(4 + 2 + 1 + 2 + 4 + 2 + 6) \div 7 = 3$

What is the median? Put the numbers in order of size and find the middle number, e.g., 1, 2, 2, 2, 4, 4, 6.

The median is 2.

What is the mode? The most common result, which is 2.

A school football team scores the following number of goals in their first 9 matches:
2, 2, 1, 3, 2, 1, 2, 4, 1

What is the mean score? 2

What is the median score? 2

Write down the mode for their results. 2

The ages of a local hockey team were:
17, 15, 16, 19, 17, 19, 22, 17, 18, 21, 17

What is the mean of their ages? 18

What is their median age? 17

Write down the mode for their ages. 17

The results of Susan's last 11 spelling tests were:
15, 12, 15, 17, 11, 16, 19, 11, 3, 11, 13

What is the mean of her scores? 13

What is her median score? 13

Write down the mode for her scores. 11

Multiplying decimals

Work out these calculations.

4.6	3.9	8.4
× 3	× 5	× 8
13.8	19.5	67.2
1	4	3

Work out these calculations.

4.7	9.1	5.8	1.7	5.1
× 3	× 3	× 3	× 2	× 2
14.1	27.3	17.4	3.4	10.2

7.4	3.6	6.5	4.2	3.8
× 2	× 4	× 4	× 2	× 2
14.8	14.4	26.0	8.4	7.6

4.2	4.7	1.8	3.4	3.7
× 4	× 4	× 5	× 5	× 5
16.8	18.8	9.0	17.0	18.5

2.5	2.4	5.3	7.2	5.1
× 5	× 6	× 7	× 8	× 9
12.5	14.4	37.1	57.6	45.9

7.9	8.6	8.8	7.5	9.9
× 9	× 9	× 8	× 8	× 6
71.1	77.4	70.4	60.0	59.4

6.8	5.7	6.9	7.5	8.4
× 7	× 6	× 7	× 9	× 9
47.6	34.2	48.3	67.5	75.6

7.3	2.8	3.8	7.7	9.4
× 8	× 7	× 8	× 7	× 9
58.4	19.6	30.4	53.9	84.6

Multiplying decimals

Work out these calculations.

37.5	26.2	65.3
× 2	× 5	× 9
75.0	131.0	587.7
1 1	3 1	4 2

Work out these calculations.

53.3	93.2	51.4	34.6	35.2
× 2	× 2	× 2	× 3	× 3
106.6	186.4	102.8	103.8	105.6

46.5	25.8	16.4	47.1	37.4
× 4	× 4	× 3	× 5	× 5
186.0	103.2	49.2	235.5	187.0

12.4	46.3	17.5	36.5	72.4
× 5	× 5	× 6	× 6	× 7
62.0	231.5	105.0	219.0	506.8

37.5	20.3	73.4	92.6	47.9
× 7	× 7	× 7	× 6	× 6
262.5	142.1	513.8	555.6	287.4

53.9	75.6	28.8	79.4	99.9
× 8	× 8	× 8	× 8	× 9
431.2	604.8	230.4	635.2	899.1

37.9	14.8	35.4	46.8	27.2
× 9	× 9	× 9	× 8	× 7
341.1	133.2	318.6	374.4	190.4

39.5	84.2	68.5	73.2	47.6
× 6	× 9	× 8	× 9	× 6
237.0	757.8	548.0	658.8	285.6

p218

Real life problems

In a class of 30 children 6 children are painting.
What percentage of children are painting?
$\frac{6}{30}$ of the children are painting and
to change a fraction to a percentage
we multiply by 100.

20%

$\frac{6}{30} \times 100 = 20$

40% of a class is made up of girls. If there are
12 girls, how many children are in the class?
If 12 girls are 40% of the class, we
divide 12 by 40 to find 1%.
Then we multiply by 100 to find 100%.

30 children

$\frac{12}{40} \times 100 = 30$

A shop has 60 books by a new author. If it sells 45
of the books what percentage does it sell?

75%

$\frac{45}{60} \times 100 = 75$

A school disco sells 65% of its tickets. If it had
120 tickets to start with, how many has it sold?

78 tickets

$\frac{120}{100} \times 65 = 78$

200 people go on a school trip. If 14% are adults,
how many children go on the trip?

172 children

$100 - 14 = 86\%$
$\frac{200}{100} \times 86 = 172$

A shop sells 150 T-shirts but 12 are returned
because they are faulty. What percentage of
the T-shirts was faulty?

8%

$\frac{12}{150} \times 100 = 8$

A year group of 120 children are asked their
favourite colours.

15% like red. How many children like red? 18 $\frac{120}{100} \times 15 = 18$

20% like green. How many children like green? 24 $\frac{120}{100} \times 20 = 24$

30% like yellow. How many children like yellow? 36 $\frac{120}{100} \times 30 = 36$

35% like blue. How many children like blue? 42 $\frac{120}{100} \times 35 = 42$

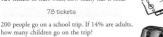

p219

Real life problems

Deborah's school bag weighs 4.67 kg.
Asha's weighs 3.98 kg. How much more does
Deborah's weigh than Asha's?

0.69 kg

$\begin{array}{r} 4.67 \\ -3.98 \\ \hline 0.69 \end{array}$

What is the total weight of the two bags?

8.65 kg

$\begin{array}{r} 4.67 \\ +3.98 \\ \hline 8.65 \end{array}$

A man wants to fit a new door. If the door frame is
2m 5cm high and the new door is 2.09 m long,
how much will he have to cut off the door?

4 cm

$\begin{array}{r} 2.09 \\ -2.05 \\ \hline .04 \end{array}$

Bert earns £14 632 a year, George earns
£24 321 a year, and Horace earns £12 971
a year. How much do they earn altogether?

£51 924

$\begin{array}{r} 14.632 \\ 24.321 \\ +12.971 \\ \hline 51.924 \end{array}$

How much more than Bert
does George earn?

£9 689

$\begin{array}{r} 24321 \\ -14632 \\ \hline 9689 \end{array}$

How much more than Horace does Bert
earn?

£1 661

$\begin{array}{r} 14632 \\ -12971 \\ \hline 1661 \end{array}$

How much more than Horace does
George earn?

£11 350

$\begin{array}{r} 24321 \\ -12971 \\ \hline 11350 \end{array}$

A lift says 'Maximum weight 270 kg'. If four people get in
weighing 72.93 kg, 47.81 kg, 85.99 kg, and 79.36 kg, by
how much are they overloading the lift?

16.09 kg

$\begin{array}{r} 72.93 \\ 47.81 \\ 85.99 \\ +79.36 \\ \hline 286.09 \end{array}$ $\begin{array}{r} 286.09 \\ -270.00 \\ \hline 16.09 \end{array}$

p220

Fraction problems

Find $\frac{3}{5}$ of £30.00.

£30.00 ÷ 5 = £6.00 $\left(\frac{1}{5}\right)$
£6.00 × 3 = £18.00 $\left(\frac{3}{5}\right)$
$\frac{3}{5}$ of £30 is £18

Find $\frac{7}{10}$ of 60 cm.

60cm ÷ 10 = 6 cm $\left(\frac{1}{10}\right)$
6 cm × 7 = 42 cm $\left(\frac{7}{10}\right)$
$\frac{7}{10}$ of 60 cm is 42 cm

Find $\frac{3}{5}$ of these amounts.

40 cm
40 ÷ 5 = 8 $\left(\frac{1}{5}\right)$
8 × 3 = 24
$\frac{3}{5}$ of 40 cm is 24 cm

£50
50 ÷ 5 = 10
10 × 3 = 30
$\frac{3}{5}$ of £50 is £30

£10.50
10.50 ÷ 5 = 2.10
2.10 × 3 = 6.30
$\frac{3}{5}$ of £10.50 is £6.30

80 m
80 ÷ 5 = 16
16 × 3 = 48
$\frac{3}{5}$ of 80 m is 48 m

75 g
75 ÷ 5 = 15
15 × 3 = 45
$\frac{3}{5}$ of 75 g is 45 g

45 kg
45 ÷ 5 = 9
9 × 3 = 27
$\frac{3}{5}$ of 45 kg is 27 kg

Find $\frac{7}{10}$ of these amounts.

48 m
48 ÷ 10 = 4.8
4.8 × 7 = 33.6
$\frac{7}{10}$ of 48 m is 33.6 m

£98.00
98 ÷ 10 = 9.8
9.8 × 7 = 68.6
$\frac{7}{10}$ of £98.00 is £68.60

75 km
75 ÷ 10 = 7.5
7.5 × 7 = 52.5
$\frac{7}{10}$ of 75 km is 52.5 km

Find $\frac{2}{3}$ of these amounts.

48 cm
48 ÷ 3 = 16
16 × 2 = 32
$\frac{2}{3}$ of 48 m is 32 m

120 kg
120 ÷ 3 = 40
40 × 2 = 80
$\frac{2}{3}$ of 120 kg is 80 kg

£24.00
24 ÷ 3 = 8
8 × 2 = 16
$\frac{2}{3}$ of £24.00 is £16.00

p221

Finding percentages

Find 30% of 140.

(Divide by 100 to find 1% and then multiply by 30 to find 30%.) $\frac{140}{100} \times 30 = 42$

Find 12% of 75. $\frac{75}{100} \times 12 = 9$

Find 30% of these numbers.

620 $\frac{620}{100} \times 30 = 186$ 240 $\frac{240}{100} \times 30 = 72$

80 $\frac{80}{100} \times 30 = 24$ 160 $\frac{160}{100} \times 30 = 48$

Find 60% of these numbers.

60 $\frac{60}{100} \times 60 = 36$ 100 $\frac{100}{100} \times 60 = 60$

160 $\frac{160}{100} \times 60 = 96$ 580 $\frac{580}{100} \times 60 = 348$

Find 45% of these amounts.

80 g $\frac{80}{100} \times 45 = 36 g$ 40 cm $\frac{40}{100} \times 45 = 18 cm$

240 ml $\frac{240}{100} \times 45 = 108 ml$ 600 km $\frac{600}{100} \times 45 = 270 km$

Find 12% of these amounts.

£150 $\frac{150}{100} \times 12 = £18$ £600 $\frac{600}{100} \times 12 = £72$

125 m $\frac{125}{100} \times 12 = 15 m$ 775 m $\frac{775}{100} \times 12 = 93 m$

p222 More algebra

Work out this equation.

$10 - a = a$
$10 - a(+a) = a(+a)$
$10 = 2a$
$10(\div 2) = 2a(\div 2)$
$a = 5$

$3b + 15 = 12 * 6$
$3b + 15(-15) = 72(-15)$
$3b = 57$
$3b(\div 3) = 57(\div 3)$
$b = 19$

$27 \div c = 9$
$27 \div c(\times c) = 9(\times c)$
$27 = 9c$
$27(\div 9) = 9c(\div 9)$
$3 = c$

Find value of each letter.

$5a = 25$	$a = 5$	$15 \div c = 5$	$c = 3$
$a = 36 - a$	$a = 18$	$32 \div c = 8$	$c = 4$
$6a = 42$	$a = 7$	$56 \div c = 7$	$c = 8$
$3y + 8 = 20$	$y = 4$	$d \div 4 = 7$	$d = 28$
$6y - 16 = 38$	$y = 9$	$d \div 9 = 5$	$d = 45$
$42 - 5y = 22$	$y = 4$	$d \div 11 = 10$	$d = 110$

Solve these equations.

$56 - a = 26 + 2a$	$a = 10$	$48 \div d = 7 + 5$	$d = 4$
$2b + 16 = (12 \times 3) - 2$	$b = 9$	$17 + c = 26 - 2c$	$c = 3$
$4y - 27 = 72 \div 8$	$y = 9$	$4e + 45 = 35 + 6e$	$e = 5$

Write equations for these problems and then solve them.

Isla bought two packets of biscuits and a 20 pence bunch of bananas. The total cost was 80 pence. How much is one pack of biscuits? $2b + 20 = 80$ 50 $b = 30$

Jodie invited 48 guests to her New Year party. 10 people couldn't make it and half of the rest were going to arrive late. How many were going to be on time? $48 = 10 + 2g$ 50 $g = 19$

p223 Multiplication by tens and units

Work out the answer to each calculation.

```
  527          834
x  76        x  58
36 890       41 700
 3 162        6 672
40 052       48 372
```

Work out the answer to each calculation.

```
  426     895     632     778
x  84   x  65   x  39   x  49
34 080  53 700  18 960  31 120
 1 704   4 475   5 688     702
35 784  58 175  24 648  38 122

  597     994     632     747
x  46   x  37   x  64   x  75
23 880  29 820  37 920  52 290
 3 582   6 958   2 528   3 735
27 462  36 778  40 448  56 025

  428     147     236     145
x  95   x  62   x  87   x  33
38 520   8 820  18 880   4 350
 2 140     294   1 652     435
40 660   9 114  20 532   4 785

  346     529     485     763
x  85   x  72   x  29   x  84
27 680  37 030   9 700  61 040
 1 730   1 058   4 365   3 052
29 410  38 088  14 065  64 092
```

p224 Naming parts of a circle

Label the part of this circle.

radius

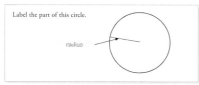

Choose from the following words to label these circles:
radius, diameter, centre, arc, sector, quadrant

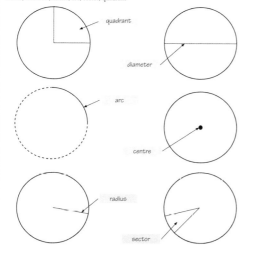

quadrant

diameter

arc

centre

radius

sector

p225 Area of right-angled triangles

Find the area of this right-angled triangle.

Because the area of this triangle is half the area of the rectangle shown, we can find the area of the rectangle and then divide it by two to find the area of the triangle.
So the area = (8 cm * 4 cm) ÷ 2
= 32 ÷ 2 = 16 cm²

Area = 16 cm²

Find the areas of these right-angled triangles.

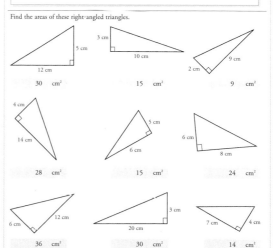

30 cm²   15 cm²   9 cm²

28 cm²   15 cm²   24 cm²

36 cm²   30 cm²   14 cm²

Cubes of small numbers

2^3 means:

$2 \times 2 \times 2 = 8$

Volume is the space inside a 3D shape.

2 cm

What is the volume of this cube?

$2 \times 2 \times 2 = 8$ cm³

You find the volume of a cube in the same way as working out the cube of a number.

Use extra paper here if you need to. What is...

3^3 $3 \times 3 \times 3 = 27$ 4^3 $4 \times 4 \times 4 = 64$

6^3 $6 \times 6 \times 6 = 216$ 5^3 $5 \times 5 \times 5 = 125$

1^3 $1 \times 1 \times 1 = 1$ 2^3 $2 \times 2 \times 2 = 8$

What are the volumes of these cubes?

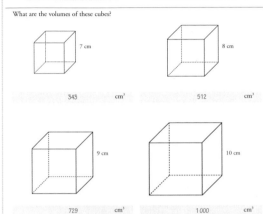

7 cm

343   cm³

8 cm

512   cm³

9 cm

729   cm³

10 cm

1 000   cm³

Cubes of larger numbers

What is 11^3?

$11 \times 11 \times 11 = 1\,331$

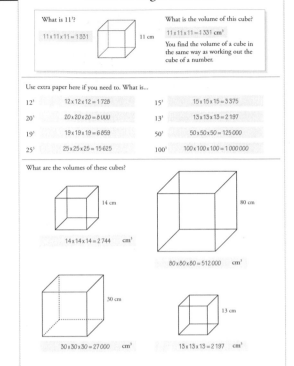

11 cm

What is the volume of this cube?

$11 \times 11 \times 11 = 1\,331$ cm³

You find the volume of a cube in the same way as working out the cube of a number.

Use extra paper here if you need to. What is...

12^3 $12 \times 12 \times 12 = 1\,728$ 15^3 $15 \times 15 \times 15 = 3\,375$

20^3 $20 \times 20 \times 20 = 8\,000$ 13^3 $13 \times 13 \times 13 = 2\,197$

19^3 $19 \times 19 \times 19 = 6\,859$ 50^3 $50 \times 50 \times 50 = 125\,000$

25^3 $25 \times 25 \times 25 = 15\,625$ 100^3 $100 \times 100 \times 100 = 1\,000\,000$

What are the volumes of these cubes?

14 cm

$14 \times 14 \times 14 = 2\,744$ cm³

80 cm

$80 \times 80 \times 80 = 512\,000$ cm³

30 cm

$30 \times 30 \times 30 = 27\,000$ cm³

13 cm

$13 \times 13 \times 13 = 2\,197$ cm³

Nets of 3D shapes

For which 3D shape is this the net?

cube

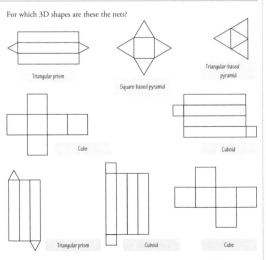

For which 3D shapes are these the nets?

Triangular prism

Square-based pyramid

Triangular-based pyramid

Cube

Cuboid

Triangular prism

Cuboid

Cube

Nets of simple shapes

Sketch the net of this cuboid.

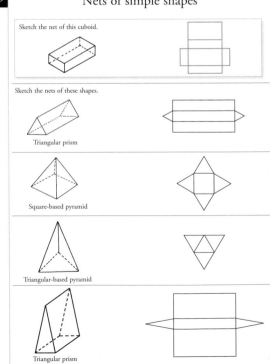

Sketch the nets of these shapes.

Triangular prism

Square-based pyramid

Triangular-based pyramid

Triangular prism

Drawing angles including reflex

Acute angles are between 0° and 90°.   Obtuse angles are between 90° and 180°.

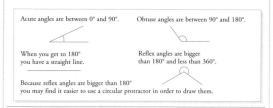

When you get to 180° you have a straight line.

Reflex angles are bigger than 180° and less than 360°.

Because reflex angles are bigger than 180° you may find it easier to use a circular protractor in order to draw them.

Use a protractor to draw these angles. Remember to mark the angle you have drawn.

150°	135°

210°	350°
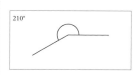	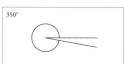
10°	20°

Drawing more angles including reflex

Draw these angles. Remember to mark the angle you have drawn.

275°	65°
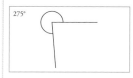	
330°	35°
	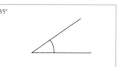
25°	345°
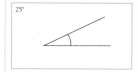	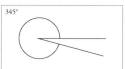
165°	5°

Drawing 2D shapes

Congruent shapes are shapes that have angles and sides of exactly the same size.

These shapes are congruent because they can be fitted exactly on top of each other.

Measure the angles and sides of these shapes and draw a congruent shape next to each one.

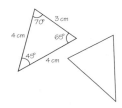
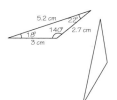

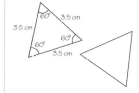
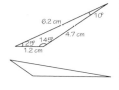

Coordinates

Write the coordinates of:

A   (2, 4)

B   (3, 1)

C   (1, 1)

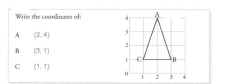

Write the coordinates of:

A (2, 9)	B (4, 11)	C (6, 9)	D (4, 6)	E (10, 9)
F (15, 9)	G (13, 7)	H (8, 7)	I (3, 5)	J (4, 4)
K (4, 3)	L (3, 2)	M (2, 2)	N (1, 3)	O (1, 4)
P (2, 5)	Q (8, 5)	R (15, 5)	S (15, 2)	T (8, 2)

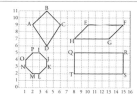

Plot these points on the grid, and join them up in the right order.

(0, 1) (1, 3) (3, 3) (5, 1) (0, 1). What shape does this make?   Trapezium

(3, 6) (4, 7) (9, 2) (8, 1) (3, 6). What shape does this make?   Rectangle

(11, 3) (13, 5) (15, 3) (13, 1) (11, 3). What shape does this make?   Square

253

INDEX

2D shapes 17, 178, 196, 232
3D shapes 178, 179, 197, 228

A

add 164, 176, 206
adjective 37, 62–63, 67, 101,
    123, 142
    comparatives 66–67
    superlatives 66–67
adverbials 82–83
adverbs 64–65, 82, 101
angles 180–181, 182–183,
    191, 197, 230–231, 232
antonym 124–125
apostrophes 102–103, 127, 133
    possessive 103, 133
area 199, 208, 225
attitude 20
averages 186, 187, 188

B

brackets 176, 209
bullet points 132

C

capacity (volume) 199, 208,
    226–227
capital letter 50, 76, 77, 78,
    79, 96, 105, 147
circle 192, 224
classic novel 36, 38
clause 47, 84–89, 90, 100, 145
    main 86–97, 145
    relative 89, 90
    subordinate 88, 145

colon 104, 127, 128–129
commas 100–101, 126
conjunctions 70, 71, 85, 88
co-ordinates 184–185, 233
cubes 197, 226–227

D

decimals 170–171, 206, 210,
    212, 216–217
determiners 74–75
diet 13
divide 158, 168–169, 176,
    187, 211, 212

E

ellipses 130
equations 192–193, 205,
    222
estimation 157
exclamation mark 78, 79,
    99
exercise 12, 16

F

factors 158–159, 200
feedback 21
fiction 24
formulas 194–195, 199
fractions 164–169,
    173, 175, 191, 198,
    201–203, 220
    adding 164, 201
    dividing 168, 203
    multiplying 166, 202
    subtracting 165, 201

G

grammar test 47, 49
graph 184, 188–189
    line graphs 188–189

H

height 157, 189, 208
homophones 46, 48, 134

I

indices (orders) 176
interjections 72–73
inverted commas (speech marks)
    94–95, 101, 126, 147

L

learning styles 18–19
length 199, 208
letter 34–35, 139

M

mass 199
maths test 150–151
    methods 152
    workings 152
mean 186, 187, 215
median 186, 215
metaphor 37
mnemonics 112
mode 186, 215
multiples 160–161, 200
multiplication tables 198–199
multiply 160, 166–167, 176,
    198–199, 210, 216, 217, 223
myth 28

N

nets 178–179, 228–229
non-fiction 24, 43
nouns 33, 62, 74, 80, 101, 123
   abstract 51
   proper 50
numbers
   negative 154–155, 207
   positive 154–155

O

onomatopoeia 43
order of operations 176–177

P

paragraph 39, 147
parenthesis 131
percentages 172–173, 175,
   191, 213, 218, 221
perimeter 199, 208
personification 141
phonics 46
phrases 80, 81
   noun phrases 80
   prepositional phrase 81
pie charts 190–191
poetry 24, 32–33, 141
polygons 182–183, 185
points of view 140
prefix 46, 121, 122, 125
prepositions 68–69, 81
prime numbers 162–163,
   198, 200
problem solving 151, 208,
   213, 218–219
pronouns 47, 52–53
   relative 90
proportion 175, 204
protractor 180–181
punctuation 46, 47, 126–127, 147

Q

question mark 77, 98

R

ratio 174, 204
reading test 24–25
reading together 17, 26–27
relaxation 14–15
rhetorical question 35
rhyme 107, 135
root word 121, 122
rounding 156–157, 171

S

scales 214
semi-colon 105, 127, 128–129
sentences 76–78, 83, 86,
   92–93, 96–99, 128–129,
   130–131, 144–145
   active 92–93, 146
   commands 79
   exclamation 78
   passive 92–93, 146
   questions 77
   statement 76
sequences 194–195
silent consonants 120
simile 37
sleep 12, 16
speech
   direct 94, 101, 136, 147
   formal 138–139
   informal 138–139
   reported 95, 137
   speech marks 94–95, 101,
      126, 147
spelling
   patterns 47, 48, 108–109
   techniques 49, 106–119
   test 46

subtract 164, 176
suffix 46, 121, 123
synonym 142–143

T

teaching methods 20
temperature 188
traditional story 30–31
triangles 196, 225

V

venn diagram 160
verbs 54–61, 84, 91, 92,
   93, 123
   future 55
   infinitive 60–61
   past 54
   perfect 58–59
   present 54
   progressive 56–57

W

word art 118

ACKNOWLEDGEMENTS

Dorling Kindersley would like to thank Acute Graphics for their illustrations pp. 154-195.
Contains public sector information licensed under the Open Government Licence v3.0,
which can be found on the National Archives website and accessed via the following link:
www.nationalarchives.gov.uk/doc/open-government-licence

The publisher would like to thank the following for their kind permission to reproduce their photographs:
(Key: a-above; b-below/bottom; c-centre; f-far; l-left; r-right; t-top)

10 123RF.com: Cathy Yeulet (bc). **12 123RF.com:** Aleksandr Markin (br). **17 Getty Images:** TEK IMAGE (c). **25 123RF.com:** Oleksandr Sokolov (bc). **46 Alamy Stock Photo:** David Page (cr). **50 123RF.com:** PaylessImages (cb). **51 Dorling Kindersley:** Paul Wilkinson (bl). **Dreamstime.com:** Photoeuphoria (crb). **Fotolia:** Pei Ling Hoo (br). **52 123RF. com:** Irina Schmidt (bl). **53 123RF.com:** Luca Mason (cb). **Dreamstime.com:** Akulamatiau (cla); Picsfive (crb). **54 Dorling Kindersley:** Peter Anderson (crb). **Dreamstime.com:** Dmitry Kalinovsky (clb); Tamara Bauer (bc); Tashka2000 (br). **55 Dorling Kindersley:** Stuart's Bikes (bl). **Dreamstime.com:** Syda Productions (br); Tinnakorn Srivichai (ca). **Getty Images:** Stocktrek RF (cra). **56 Dreamstime.com:** Duncan Noakes (crb). **57 Alamy Stock Photo:** D. Hurst (cra). **Dreamstime.com:** Viktor Pravdica (ca). **58 123RF.com:** Hongqi Zhang (cb, crb). **59 Dreamstime.com:** Aginger (cl, cr). **60 123RF.com:** stockyimages (bl). **Fotolia:** Thomas Dobner / Dual Aspect (bc). **62 Dorling Kindersley:** Blackpool Zoo, Lancashire, UK (cla). **63 123RF.com:** Alena Ozerova (bl); Oleg Sheremetyev (crb). **64 123RF.com:** PaylessImages (cr). **Alamy Stock Photo:** Image Source Plus (cl); redbrickstock. com (cra). **Dreamstime.com:** Andrius Aleksandravicius (cb/Wood game); Showface (cb). **65 Dreamstime.com:** Neil Burton (cla); Wavebreakmedia Ltd (cl). **66 123RF.com:** Irina Iglina / iglira (cla); svitac (cra). **Dorling Kindersley:** Hitachi Rail Europe (clb, bc); Jerry Young (cb). **67 123RF.com:** bennymarty (cla); smileus (cra). **Dreamstime.com:** Waldru (cr). **68 Alamy Stock Photo:** D. Hurst (c). **Dorling Kindersley:** NASA (cl). **Dreamstime.com:** Alexander Raths (ca); Ron Chapple (cr). **69 Alamy Stock Photo:** Foto Grebler (bl); Zoonar GmbH (ca); tuja66 (cra). **Dreamstime.com:** Mtkang (cr). **70 123RF.com:** Mike Price / mhprice (cra). **Alamy Stock Photo:** Zoonar GmbH (bc). **71 Alamy Stock Photo:** LJSphotography (bl). **72 Dreamstime. com:** Georgerudy (cla); Sepy67 (cra); Mihail Degteariov (bl). **73 Alamy Stock Photo:** (cla). **74 123RF.com:** Bonzami Emmanuelle / cynoclub (cb/Red fish); Visarute Angkatavanich / bluehand (crb). **Alamy Stock Photo:** Krys Bailey (cra). **Fotolia:** lucielang (cb). **75 Alamy Stock Photo:** Martin Wierink (cr). **Dreamstime.com:** Irina Papoyan (br). **76 123RF.com:** pashabo (cr). **77 123RF.com:** Eric Isselee / isselee (crb). **79 Alamy Stock Photo:** Oleksiy Maksymenko (bc). **Dreamstime.com:** Jose Manuel Gelpi Diaz (crb); Vetkit (bl). **80 Alamy Stock Photo:** Ernie Jordan (clb, cb). **81 Dreamstime.com:** Esteban Miyahira (cra). **83 123RF.com:** Paolo De Santis / archidea (c). **Dorling Kindersley:** Barnabas Kindersley (cra). **Fotolia:** Eric Isselee (cla, br). **84 123RF. com:** Matthias Ziegler (cl); tan4ikk (bl). **Dreamstime.com:** Paul Maguire (cra). **Fotolia:** Silver (br). **85 123RF.com:** Matthias Ziegler (ca). **86 123RF.com:** mariok (crb). **Alamy Stock Photo:** David Chapman (clb). **87 123RF.com:** Eric Isselee / isselee (clb). **Dreamstime.com:** Limeyrunner (cb). **88 Alamy StockPhoto:** Tetra Images (cra). **Fotolia:** Dusan Zutinic / asiana (bc). **89 Dorling Kindersley:** NASA (cra). **Getty Images:** Thomas Northcut / Photodisc (crb). **90 Dreamstime.com:** Jack Schiffer (clb). **93 Getty Images:** Science & Society Picture Library (bc). **94 Corbis:** (cra). **Dreamstime.com:** Pahham (c). **95 Dreamstime.com:** Lbarn (cb). **96 Dreamstime.com:** Natasnow (cra). **100 123RF.com:** Yury Gubin (bc). **Dorling Kindersley:** Liberty's Owl, Raptor and Reptile Centre, Hampshire, UK (crb). **101 123RF.com:** svitlana10 (cra). **104 123RF.com:** Anton Starikov (cra). **Dreamstime.com:** Douglas W Fry (crb); Rmarmion (cl). **Photolibrary:** Photodisc / Ryan McVay (ca). **105 Dreamstime.com:** Sefi Greiver (cl). **PunchStock:** Westend61 / Rainer Dittrich (crb). **106 Dreamstime.com:** Happyshoot (c). **110 Dreamstime.com:** Uros Petrovic (tl). **111 Dreamstime.com:** Uros Petrovic (tr, clb). **113 Dreamstime.com:** Marusea Turcu (tr). **114 Dorling Kindersley:** Jerry Young (tr). **Dreamstime.com:** Eric Isselee (crb).

All other images © Dorling Kindersley.
For further information see: www.dkimages.com